# WE BELIEVE

# WE
# BELIEVE

An Interpretation of the
United Church Statement of Faith

ROGER LINCOLN SHINN
AND
DANIEL DAY WILLIAMS

United Church Press
Philadelphia · Boston

# Contents

FOREWORD    7

STATEMENT OF FAITH    9

PART I. AN OVERVIEW OF THE STATEMENT    13

PART II. THE DECLARATIONS OF THE DEEDS OF GOD    35

*He Calls and Creates*    42

*He Seeks to Save*    51

*He Judges*    62

*In Jesus Christ He Has Come*    73

*He Bestows His Spirit*    87

*He Calls to Discipleship*    96

*He Promises*    108

APPENDIXES    121

*The Use of the Statement*    121

*The Development of the Statement*    123

*The Statement in Translation*    126

# Foreword

» In this book we are offering an interpretation of the Statement of Faith of the United Church of Christ, approved by the General Synod at Oberlin, Ohio, July 5–9, 1959. We have written at the invitation of the Committee on Publication of the United Church Board for Homeland Ministries. But this is in no sense an "official" book. The Statement of Faith is a public document that everyone is free to interpret. This book is one interpretation. We have sought to interpret the Statement as an expression of the mind and faith of the United Church of Christ, but of course our commentary reflects our individual convictions and ideas. We gladly recognize that others have every right to interpretations that differ from ours.

Our aim is primarily to understand the Statement, not to defend or praise it. We seek to place it in the context of Christian history and the life of the Christian church. We want to show its relation to the biblical message, to traditional doctrine, to the Christian thought of our time, and to the contemporary world. We try to point out where it takes clear stands and where it invites Christians to further thought and discussion about their faith.

We have worked together on the entire book. Every chapter shows marks of our discussions. In our common effort we divided the initial responsibilities as follows: Daniel D. Williams, the first four declarations of the Statement; Roger L. Shinn, the overview and the last three declarations.

We submit our work in the hope that it will contribute to a clearer understanding of Christian faith today and to the continuing ecumenical conversations of our time.

R.L.S.–D.D.W.

# Statement of Faith

We believe in God, the Eternal Spirit, Father of our Lord Jesus Christ and our Father, and to his deeds we testify:

He calls the worlds into being,
creates man in his own image
and sets before him the ways of life and death.

He seeks in holy love to save all people from aimlessness and sin.

He judges men and nations by his righteous will
declared through prophets and apostles.

In Jesus Christ, the man of Nazareth, our crucified and risen Lord,
he has come to us
and shared our common lot,
conquering sin and death
and reconciling the world to himself.

He bestows upon us his Holy Spirit,
creating and renewing the church of Jesus Christ,
binding in covenant faithful people of all ages,
tongues, and races.

He calls us into his church
to accept the cost and joy of discipleship,
to be his servants in the service of men
to proclaim the gospel to all the world
and resist the powers of evil,
to share in Christ's baptism and eat at his table,
to join him in his passion and victory.

9

He promises to all who trust him
forgiveness of sins and fullness of grace,
courage in the struggle for justice and peace,
his presence in trial and rejoicing,
and eternal life in his kingdom which has no end.

Blessing and honor, glory and power be unto him. Amen.

# PART I

# An Overview
# of the
# Statement

# An
# Overview
# of the
# Statement

» EVER SINCE JESUS OF NAZARETH called his first disciples, Christians have sought for ways to confess their faith. They needed to put their faith into words, both to clarify their own convictions and to tell others what had happened to them and what they believed.

The first great Christian confessional statement ever recorded came from Peter, who said to Jesus, "You are the Christ" (Mark 8:29). The New Testament includes other short declarations of faith—for example, "Jesus is Lord" (1 Cor. 12:3), and "Jesus is the Son of God" (1 John 4:15).

Such remarkable directness and brevity was sometimes enough—especially if men knew who Jesus was, what he had done, and what he had asked his followers to do. But often more had to be said. The believer had to include some of the facts about Jesus and had to explain the meaning of belief in him and faithfulness to him.

If individual Christians needed to declare their faith, the church had even stronger reasons to express the common faith that united its members. This church wanted to identify itself and to tell its message to the world. Frequently it had to seek some precision of language, in order to prevent misinterpretations that might fragment the church or confuse its beliefs with various rival beliefs. Hence the church—including many groups within the church—has often through the centuries formulated convictions in testimonies of faith.

The contemporary church, no less than the traditional church, needs to think about the meaning and the communication of its faith. Therefore churches in the twentieth century, especially in missionary situations and in times of decision, have sought to declare their faith. Thus it was that the United Church of Christ, at the beginning of its career, decided to work out a "Statement of Faith."

The two groups who formed the United Church both had rich inheritances of confessional documents. Like all Christians, they were the heirs of the ancient creeds imbedded in scripture and developed in the early centuries of the church. The Evangelical and Reformed Church had given great attention to the confessions of the Reformation. The Congregational Christian Churches had drawn upon the documents of English Puritanism and the many covenants and doctrinal statements of American Congregationalism. Now the United Church, concerned that its formation be an act of Christian faith and not simply a functional merger of denominations, took the occasion of union as an opportunity for rethinking its belief. In 1959, a year before adopting a constitution, the General Synod discussed at length and approved the Statement of Faith.

A *statement of faith*, we should clearly realize, is not *faith*. Talk about belief can be a cheap substitute or even an evasion of the trust and commitment that belong to real faith. So no Christian should exaggerate the value of confessions and creeds. Certainly nobody should assume that the faith of any church can be encompassed in its words.

But words are important. One responsibility of a church is to search its mind and to declare its convictions. A belief that is unsaid is incomplete, and a belief that is well said becomes a power for life and action. Therefore the process of thinking that led to the Statement of Faith and the continuing use of that Statement have become one significant part of the life of the United Church of Christ. And the Statement is part of that church's contribution to the conversation and life of the wider church in which it seeks to play its part.

# Statements and Creeds

Creeds often have a bad reputation in our world. The words *creedal* and *creedalism* are likely to sound reactionary. They may be associated with rigid orthodoxies, with unwillingness to face new evidence, with rest in traditionalism instead of encounter with the present.

Actually *creed* is simply the noun that comes from the verb *credo*, which means "I believe." We expect people to have beliefs. We respect the person who has the courage of his convictions—and our respect assumes that he has convictions worthy of his courage. So in the most basic sense all Christian faith has its creedal element.

But the history of creeds has its discouraging side. Men

have burned their neighbors at the stake on creedal grounds. Sometimes the most thoughtful and intelligent persons have been barred from the church because they questioned its creeds, while lethargic churchmen went on reciting the creeds without any trouble. Servants of Christ, living in his spirit, have been persecuted by spiteful people who fanatically held to every article in an inherited creed.

The United Church of Christ, aware of this history, chose to develop a Statement of Faith rather than a creed. In the most technical sense, perhaps there is no difference between the two. But "statement of faith" suggests a less rigid, less authoritarian document than "creed." Perhaps it suggests also a more modest attempt to say what it is that contemporary Christians believe.

In any case the Statement of Faith is not a standard of objective authority in the United Church. Whatever authority it has is the authority of an honest testimony with the persuasiveness of its contents. Long before its adoption the decision had been made that this Statement would be "a testimony, and not a test, of faith."[1]

In the usage of the United Church, *testimony* represents both less and more than a test. It represents less in terms of a legal standard. The Statement of Faith will not be the occasion for any heresy trials. No one will be excluded from the church or denied ordination because of disagreement with it.

In a shrewd theological observation Ogden Nash once wrote:

> There are too many people who think that
> just because they have parishes or dioceses
> It imparts infallibility to all their biases.

[1] The phraseology comes from the *Basis of Union* of the Congregational Christian Churches and the Evangelical and Reformed Church, p. 4, n. 3, and p. 6. This document represented the agreement upon which the United Church was organized, prior to the writing of the constitution of this church.

The structure of the United Church has no place for claims of human infallibility. And this church makes no pretense that it has discovered once and for all the right way to state the core of Christian belief. Thus its testimony of faith is less than a test.

But a testimony is also far more than a test. A testimony involves a commitment. Many a person who could pass a test in doctrine cannot make a testimony of faith, because he lacks the courage and the joy of faith. The Statement of Faith is an effort to find a language appropriate for Christian testimony.

Consistent with this whole conception, the Statement of Faith has no legal status in the United Church. The General Synod "approved" it and "submitted" it to the conferences, associations, and local churches of the United Church, not for their ratification but for their approval and use. The General Synod further "encouraged" use of the Statement "in congregational worship, in private devotions, and for purposes of study." It has been used in all these ways, but the United Church of Christ nowhere requires its use.[2]

A testimony, someone has observed, is in the last analysis inevitably a test. Perhaps this is so—in the sense that every day and every activity of life tests faith, love, and purposes. A church in declaring and living by its faith is putting itself to the test. But the Statement of Faith, as a testimony of Christian conviction, is adding to life no test that is not inherent in Christian existence.

William Temple, the great Archbishop of Canterbury of the generation just past, once wrote: "I do not believe in any creed, but I use certain creeds to express, to conserve, and to deepen my belief in God."[3] The language of belief is important. But the belief is not in the language; it is in God. Consistent with that idea, the Statement of Faith uses the word *believe* only once. It begins, "We believe in God." It does not even

[2] See Appendixes, "The Use of the Statement."
[3] *Nature, Man and God* (London: Macmillan, 1934), p. 322.

assert *belief in* creation, in the church, in the forgiveness of sins, in eternal life; rather it testifies to all these as deeds of God. The *belief*—a word which in Protestant Christianity is closely related to *trust*—is in God. (See pages 35–37.)

# Tradition and Contemporaneity

The Christian community lives in every generation with a memory of the past and a destiny in the future. The present, the time of responsibility, gets its meaning from a heritage of history and an expectation of history yet to come. Built into the meaning of the church are a loyalty to its ancient sources and a conviction of a mission that is uncompleted. Therefore the church by its very nature must maintain a sensitivity to a tradition that has made it and a contemporaneous task that is still making it.

The United Church of Christ, even before writing its Statement of Faith, had considered with some care the meaning for faith of the tug of tradition and the tug of contemporaneity. The uniting communions had already voted their approval of the following statement: "The faith which unites us and to which we bear witness is that faith in God which the Scriptures of the Old and New Testaments set forth, which the ancient church expressed in the ecumenical creeds, to which our own spiritual fathers gave utterance in the evangelical confessions of the Reformation, and which we are in duty bound to express in the words of our time as God himself gives us light."[4]

Since the interplay of tradition and contemporaneity is so important to Christian faith, let us examine briefly each of these forces in turn.

[4] *Basis of Union*, p. 4.

*Christian faith comes to us through a tradition.* This faith arose almost twenty centuries ago in a response to historical events centering in Jesus of Nazareth, whom men recognized as the Christ (meaning Messiah or Lord). That history is recorded in a Bible, written long ago. The process of formulating Christian beliefs began in the Bible and continued in the life of the church. In its first five centuries the church developed several declarations of its faith. These grew out of a combination of informal and formal processes, as Christians responded to their own needs, to challenges from outside the church, and to debates within the church.

The most famous of the ancient confessions of faith is called the Apostles' Creed. It developed gradually in the Western church, taking preliminary form in the third century and its present form by about A.D. 600. Other creeds are associated with councils where Christians argued the meaning of their faith and carefully hammered out formulas to declare and guard its substance. The most important of these councils were the Council of Nicaea, A.D. 325,[5] and the Council of Chalcedon, A.D. 451.

This process continued through the centuries with many variations in different parts of the church. Through it all we see the working of tradition. Wrongly understood, tradition can be the dead weight of the past, stifling the present. But in its original meaning tradition (rooted in the Latin verb *tradere*) is the activity that passes on the experiences and insights of the past to the present and future.

The Christian church does not originate a new faith in each age. It confesses the faith of prophets, apostles, and martyrs in

[5] The creed that is usually called the Nicene Creed and that is often used in Christian worship is not actually the creed that came out of the Council of Nicaea. It is a later, more comprehensive creed that includes some phrases from the Council of Nicaea. For convenience we shall follow the common use and call it the Nicene Creed throughout this book.

its past. Repeatedly in times of persecution and temptation its loyalty to traditional faith has saved it from cheap compromises and apostasy. Yet adherence to the past can never shield anyone from the demands of life in the present. Therefore the church must constantly think about the relation between tradition and contemporaneity.

*Christian faith is contemporary.* It arose among men who responded to a Lord who refused to be imprisoned by any past and whose followers often had to break with the past. It discovered that the Word of God, so powerfully set forth in books, could not be confined to unchanging words. This Word, in the fullness of time, was no longer simply words; it was the Word made flesh, the Word that lived among us, full of grace and truth (John 1:14). It was—and is—"living and active, sharper than any two-edged sword" (Heb. 4:12).

In the record of the Gospel According to John, Jesus told his disciples that the Holy Spirit would *both* recall to them what he (Jesus) had taught *and* teach them all things (John 14:26). Similarly he said that his followers would *both* do what he had done *and* go on to greater works (John 14:12). Clearly that loyalty to tradition, far from freezing us in the past, requires that we live, think, and act in the present.

As we look at the creeds of the past, whether in the Bible or in the centuries following its writing, we find always an interaction of the traditional and the contemporary. The declaration tells of something *given*, something that has happened, something that is not the achievement of the persons who report it. But the thought and language of the declaration are the work of men living in their own present, using the language and concepts of their time, yet challenging their own time. What they did, we now must do. We cannot simply rest contented with their work. The restatement of Christian faith is a task and opportunity for every generation. We are "in duty bound" to exercise that privilege today.

Tradition and contemporaneity usually exist in some tension. Today especially we are likely to feel that tension. A scientific age understands things as no past age did. Our picture of the world, our concepts, our mental processes often are radically different from those of men who wrote the Bible. Christian thinking demands both effort and imagination, as it seeks to appreciate an ancient or alien insight and yet be honest in its modern apprehension of things. Sometimes the church seems to be torn between a backward pull of the Bible and a forward pull of history, forced to make an unhappy choice or an equally unhappy compromise between the two.

It would be too glib to say that no such issue arises in the Statement of Faith. It has prompted many a discussion between those especially sensitive to the Christian heritage and those especially responsive to our time. Some of those issues will be mentioned in the commentary on various articles of the Statement later in this book.

Yet for the most part the Statement has not led to a clash between the faith set forth in scripture and the words of our time. The reason lies in a discovery—perhaps the right word is revelation—that has come into the experience of Christians repeatedly in history, never more remarkably than in our own time. It is the experience of a scripture that does not pull them to the past but drives them into the midst of life today. When Christians get closer to the great scriptural declarations, they get closer to themselves. The Word of God, addressing them through the Bible, breaks through the hardened religious formulas and patterns of past and present alike.

Such a claim may seem to be merely a pious generalization —and no doubt it could be repeated as such. But its meaning becomes clearer in one specific characteristic of the Statement.

# The Deeds
# of God

The most distinctive quality of the Statement of Faith, as compared with the classical creeds, appears immediately in the way it is constructed and printed. It begins with a confession of belief and ends with a doxology. Between beginning and ending come seven sentences, each telling of an activity of God. In each of these sentences the subject is the pronoun for God; the verb or verbs tell of something that God has done and is doing.

By contrast most of the traditional confessions of the church are set in a triadic form derived from the doctrine of the Trinity.[6] They contain three declarations or paragraphs concerning Father, Son, and Holy Spirit. Statements about the church, the Christian life, and other items are either associated with the third article or are grouped in a fourth.

This time-honored method provides one way of stating the Christian faith. It has been used long enough and effectively enough that it does not have to be defended. But it is not the only way. And it is not the characteristic biblical way.

The Bible itself is primarily a narrative. It is not a systematic treatise on Christian beliefs. Rather it is a record of the deeds of God and the history of a people, beginning with the creation, running through centuries of history, and concluding with an imaginative look into the future. While the Bible certainly includes doctrinal comments, law, prophecy, and devotional writing, all these are incorporated in the historical framework.

Furthermore the Bible includes several confessional statements that declare the biblical faith in a brief, concentrated

[6] For a discussion of the Trinitarian aspect of the Statement, see pp. 40–42.

way. Recent scholarship has located some of these and has shown their importance in the structure of the Bible. They are among the earliest biblical passages. They took their form in the setting of acts of worship or in the communications that first told people about Christian faith. Then in the course of the years other elements of the Bible—memories, traditions, collections of sayings, rituals, and prayers—were gathered around the basic declarations and were written down. The unique quality of the core confessional statements is that they, like the Bible as a whole, are basically testimonies to what has happened. They take a narrative form. They are recitals of the deeds of God among men.

In the Old Testament perhaps the most ancient and significant of these confessional liturgies is found in Deuteronomy 26:5–10.[7] As Gerhard von Rad has shown, it probably goes back to a time before David, perhaps even to the time of Joshua, long before the writing of the book of Deuteronomy, in which it is now included. It is the confession of faith made by the worshiper when he presents the firstfruits of the harvest.[8] It reads:

> " 'A wandering Aramean was my father; and he went down into Egypt and sojourned there, few in number; and there he became a nation, great, mighty, and populous. And the Egyptians treated us harshly, and afflicted us, and laid upon us hard bondage. Then we cried to the Lord the God of our fathers, and the Lord heard our voice, and saw our affliction, our toil, and our oppression; and the Lord brought us out of Egypt with a mighty hand and an outstretched arm, with great terror, with signs and wonders; and he brought us into this place and gave us this land, a land flowing with milk and honey. And behold, now I bring the first of the fruit of the ground, which thou, O Lord, hast given me.' "
>
> —Deuteronomy 26:5–10

[7] For comparable confessions see Deuteronomy 6:21–25 and Joshua 24:17–18.

[8] Gerhard von Rad, *Old Testament Theology*, trans. D. M. G. Stalker (New York: Harper and Row, 1962), I, 121–25.

That statement of faith is vivid, immediate, in some ways naïve. It is concerned with the experience of the individual and his ancestors. The people who used it were not yet greatly concerned about some of the wider questions—the relation of their God to the Egyptians and the many other peoples of the world, the creation of the world, the issues of justice and mercy. Eventually a mature faith would have to be more comprehensive in its scope. But already, in this very early declaration, the basic pattern of scriptural declaration was set. The confession told what had happened. It described the doings of God in the history of a people.

If we turn to the New Testament, we find that the first four books are called Gospels. These were not the first four books to be written down, but they rightly became the first books of the New Testament. A gospel is a news report—literally, good news. The four Gospels and the Acts of the Apostles, which together make up more than half of the New Testament, are a record of events—events centering in the life of Christ and the early years of the Christian church. They tell what God was doing among his people.

Within the New Testament, as within the Old, are some of the core declarations of faith. Their content is known, in the technical language of biblical scholars, as the *kerygma*. (That Greek word originally referred to the cry of a herald; it came to stand for preaching, not in the sense of a Sunday morning activity but in the sense of the telling of the Christian message.) The kerygma stated in some of the sermons in the book of Acts. Good examples are the sermons of Peter in Acts 2:14–36 and 3:12–26 and of Stephen in Acts 7:2–53. Again the message is a testimony about events, about the acts of God among his people. This kerygma, New Testament scholars widely hold, became the framework for the writing of the Gospels.

The United Church Statement of Faith, in its basic structure, follows the pattern of the biblical declarations, rather than of the typical creeds of later Christian history. It abandons the triadic form (although keeping the testimony to Father, Son, and Holy Spirit) and returns to the kerygmatic account of the deeds of God.

Thus the accented words in the Statement are the verbs that tell of God's deeds: He *creates, seeks, judges, has come* and *shared, bestows, calls, promises*. In this respect the Statement is akin both to the Bible, with its emphasis on history and divine activity, and to contemporary thought, with its affirmations of venture and activity. It is possible that traditional theology, in its Greek and Latin formulations, overemphasized static concepts and states of being. Perhaps the modern mind, taught by science that the real nature of matter is kinetic (or dynamic) rather than static, is more attuned at this point to the dynamism of scripture.

In another respect the Statement of Faith suggests an affinity between biblical and contemporary thinking. The Bible, although its language is often symbolic and poetic, is not a highly speculative book. It sticks to the record—and, of course, the meaning of the record for faith; it does not try to fill out a whole metaphysic or picture of the universe, as some Christian theologies have done. The classical creeds in their brevity do not indulge in elaborate speculations, although sometimes they reflect theologies that do. The Statement of Faith, as Harold K. Schilling has written, shows the tendency "to return . . . to the more primitive confessional affirmations of the early church, and thus to focus attention upon the basic Christian creed, and to eliminate from it as much as possible the philosophical, metaphysical, theoretical constructions that do not belong there."[9]

Certainly the Statement, by its affirmation of belief in a God who acts, is aiming to describe reality—and that is the aim of metaphysics. Furthermore, the Statement in no sense

[9] Harold K. Schilling, *Science and Religion* (New York: Charles Scribner's Sons, 1962), p. 135.

forbids further metaphysical thinking; and it has implications for a metaphysics that gives an important place to movement and activity. But it makes a few affirmations and leaves many questions open for further elaboration. Like the Bible, it reports —and lets the record speak.

# The Content of the Statement

Whenever a church tries to put its faith into words, it says some things and leaves the rest unsaid. There are two reasons that demand a rigorous process of decision about what to include and what to omit.

The first reason is that Christian faith is far too rich, subtle, and many-faceted to be communicated in any one way. It can never be reduced entirely to words; and of those aspects that can be verbalized, only some can be stated on any single occasion. When the occasion calls for a short statement that can be read aloud by a worshiping congregration, the limitations are severe. The question becomes, What in this faith is so fundamental that it must be said when all the rest is left out?

The second reason is that the faith of a church is different in some ways from the faith of an individual. A church includes persons with many opinions, even about important matters of belief. A church decides to speak forthrightly on some questions; on others it deliberately keeps open the conversation among its members. Any Christian's personal creed is likely to include important testimonies and ideas that he cannot impose upon the church. The church appreciates such diversity of ideas, even while it looks for the unity in its faith. When the church declares its faith, it seeks to formulate not the least common denominator of the beliefs within it but rather the fundamental core of conviction that unifies the church at its best.

We have already seen that the distinctive character of the Statement of Faith, as compared with most traditional doctrinal statements, is that it takes the form of a declaration of the acts of God. This form determines in large part the content. For example, the Statement does not include a confession of sin, because sin is an act of man; it does include the affirmation that God both judges sin and seeks to save men from their sin. On every subject that comes into the Statement, the accent is on what Christian faith understands God to be doing about that subject.

There is another obvious contrast between this Statement and the classical creeds. The latter concentrate on doctrine; this statement, while affirming the major Christian doctrines, gives a primary emphasis also to God's demands and promises in regard to the Christian life. In this respect, as in its structure, the Statement is akin to scripture, which in both Old and New Testaments gives great attention to the issues of faithful living. In view of this notable emphasis of the Bible, whether in the law or the prophets or in the teachings of Jesus and the apostles, it is surprising that the classical confessions have said so little on the issue.

Certainly any confession of faith that speaks to our time must say something about the expression of faith in the practical decisions of personal and social life. Throughout the history of the church, the powerful confessions of faith have usually arisen out of situations of conflict and crisis. The ancient ecumenical creeds often came out of struggles against heresies that distorted the faith and threatened the unity of the church. Today, we may judge, the temptations that threaten the church are less the doctrinal heresies of the past than the modern heresies that infiltrate the church with nationalism, racialism, and complacent culture-religion. Hence it becomes important that the church, confessing its faith, return to the biblical emphasis upon faithful discipleship.

The accent on ethics is not a separate item or an addendum to the Statement; as in scripture, it is an integral part of the meaning of faith. Thus the Statement declares that God seeks in holy love to save all people, that the Holy Spirit binds in covenant people of all races. It declares the judgment of God's righteous will. It reminds the churchman that God calls him to the service of men, that the sacraments are indissolubly related to costly commitment, that courage in the struggle for peace and justice is as truly God's gift as is eternal life. Faith and works are not opposed, but the meaning of obedience is stated in the context of the gospel of grace and forgiveness. In this respect, as in the structure of recital, the Statement seeks to maintain its kinship to both its biblical sources and the contemporary mind.

A final quality of the Statement is its ecumenical purpose. It does not intend to state the peculiar faith of the people who came together in the United Church of Christ; it aims to state the Christian faith as this church, in conversation with other groups of Christians, apprehends that faith.

Yet those who use it know that it has the limitations of the historical experiences of a small segment of mankind in our specific time. It is one way, hopefully an authentic and helpful way but certainly not the only way, to declare the Christian faith.

The General Synod of the United Church, in approving the Statement, said that it was to be "understood as a testimony of the United Church of Christ to the faith commonly held among us in the words of our time and not as a substitute for or revision of the ecumenical creeds and the confessions, platforms, and covenants of the communions joined in the United Church of Christ." The United Church was not so foolish as to try to "patch up" or modernize the traditional creeds. Because those older statements still stand and speak with power, this church decided not to imitate them but to state the traditional faith freshly. The church could risk a different style of declaration, because it knew that its limitations would be corrected by the continuing power of tradition, by conversations with other Christians today, and by insights of future generations of Christians.

## The Language
## of the Statement

Christian faith has always known the importance of language. Although the Word of God is not merely words, yet words are instruments of communication. The experience of speaking and hearing permeates the Bible. Words without deeds are empty, but words may tell of deeds and lead to deeds. Sometimes a word is a deed.

There can be no infallible taste, no absolute accuracy in language, because words say different things to different people. Yet the choice of words is utterly important. Mark Twain once said that the difference between the right word and the almost right word is the difference between lightning and the lightning bug.

The judgment as to how well the Statement of Faith found the right words must depend upon the test of continuous usage. All that can be said here is that every word in it represents a decision to use that word rather than an alternative. Many of its words were chosen after hours of study and discussion, sometimes after debate on the floor of the General Synod.

Comments on the Statement have described it both as poetic and as prosaic. Some critics find in it biblical cadences; others find "Madison Avenue language." It is clearly not a poem. Although it is printed in a semi-poetic style, this serves to indicate its structure rather than to make claims for its literary form. Insofar as its words and rhythms resemble poetry, its style is free and contemporary rather than traditional.

Four characteristics of the language deserve some comment here.

First, the language is simple. This does not mean that the meaning of all the statements is simple. The language of faith involves a profundity that calls for continuous thinking. But the sentences are direct in style. The seven declarations all involve the same structure: a subject—God—and a verb, indicating an activity of God. And the words are usually clear and plain. After the statement had taken form, someone got the idea of making a word count; his tabulation showed 159 words of one syllable, fifty-six words of two syllables, fifteen words of three syllables, and two words of four syllables.

Second, the language is not always literal. The language of faith includes symbols and metaphors. It uses the words of ordinary experience to point to extraordinary experience, the words of sensory impressions to describe realities that transcend the senses. The Statement represents an effort to speak directly and honestly—to avoid declaring beliefs that people really do not hold. But inevitably it uses symbolic language. For example, in using the biblical description of God as Father, it recognizes (as does the Bible) that it is using a common human relationship to point to a relationship that is more than human. When it says that God "calls the worlds" and "calls us," it makes human speech a metaphor for a divine activity that is in many ways unlike human talk.[10]

Third, the language is contemporary. It avoids Latinisms and Elizabethan forms that are no longer current. At the same time, because it is the document of a church, it seeks to avoid any vocabulary that is specifically associated with any single theologian or school of thought. As a result most of the words are fairly common words in contemporary speech. Some—like "aimlessness"—may be plain and prosaic, because they refer to plain and prosaic facts.

[10] For further discussion of this phraseology see pp. 42–45.

Fourth, the language often comes directly from the Bible. Biblical and contemporary expressions sometimes coincide, sometimes not. The Statement uses "reconciling," which is both biblical and contemporary, rather than "atoning," which is biblical but rarely contemporary (except in theology). Every sentence recalls the thought and language of the Bible. The Statement begins with phrases from the first book in the Bible and ends with phrases from the last book. The opening confession recalls the "Spirit" of God that moved over the face of the waters at creation, and the first declaration takes over language from Genesis 1. The concluding words of praise come from Revelation 5:13.

That final doxology is an interesting example of the language of faith. It does not follow the exact wording of either the Authorized Version (King James Version) or of the Revised Standard Version of the Bible. Yet it is more familiar than either. It is the wording from the English translation of Handel's *Messiah*. In its musical setting it belongs to the conscious or unconscious awareness of countless Christians. Coming at the end of the Statement of Faith, it is a reminder of the comment of John Calvin (and many another after him) that a creed should be sung rather than said. Whether or not we literally sing it, a confession of faith is an act of worship —a testimony rather than a test of faith.

# PART II

# The Declarations of the Deeds of God

# The Declarations
# of the
# Deeds of God

*We believe in God, the Eternal Spirit, Father
of our Lord Jesus Christ and our Father, and
to his deeds we testify:*

» BELIEVING IN GOD is an act of
faith. It includes the conviction of the mind, but it arises from
the trust and assent of the whole person. We Christians do not
just believe some things about God, we believe in him as the
one upon whom all things depend for their being and the
meaning of their existence. In this Statement of Faith we begin by acknowledging who God is as we know him through
Jesus Christ. We can speak of God as Spirit, as Father, and as
one to whose deeds we can testify, insofar as our faith is born

out of personal response to God's self-revelation which came to its climax in the story of Jesus. Certainly every creature on earth may have some sense of dependence upon a superior power. Men have acknowledged God as the source, or ground, or creator of the world in many different religions. The Statement does not deny knowledge of God to anyone who truly seeks him. But it does affirm that when we speak as Christians we find the answer to the question "Who is God?" in the history which has given rise to our faith in the Father of our Lord Jesus Christ.

This view that God makes himself known in history opens the way for us to interpret man's long search for an adequate conception of God. Many ideas of God have had to be shattered in the history of religions that a larger truth might emerge, and there are still great differences in the way God is conceived in the great religions.

Atheism, the denial of God's reality, can be understood in part as a protest against false ideas of God. Friedrich Nietzsche's declaration that God must be killed that man may be free has within it an element of protest against the kind of religion which gives man too little creative freedom. But we can also see the demonic will-to-power in Nietzsche's announcement of the death of God that the way may be opened for the superman.

At times belief in God appears so bound up with conventional religious forms which have lost their meaning that some are driven to search for the meaning of life in the secular world without any conscious belief in God. The Christian interpretation of this experience of being without God includes the insight that God does not make himself obvious. The Bible never speaks of God's presence as something to be taken for granted, but always as a truth to be confessed and a wonder to be celebrated.

When I look at thy heavens, the
work of thy fingers,
the moon and the stars which
thou hast established;
what is man that thou art mindful
of him?

—Psalm 8:3–4

Belief in God can be defended by reason but it cannot be compelled by argument. There are those for whom belief in God is a clear and sustaining fact in all of life. There are others for whom belief in God is an affirmation in the face of radical questions, a light shining in the midst of darkness. Both kinds of believers can recognize that God is more than our systems of belief about him. He reveals himself in concrete personal life, and we acknowledge his presence and his power.

*Who is God?* The Statement of Faith declares who God is before it speaks about his calling the worlds into being. This is an interesting change from the form of the Apostles' and Nicene Creeds in which God is immediately acknowledged as "the Father Almighty, maker of heaven and earth." In speaking first of God as Father of our Lord Jesus Christ, the Statement reflects accurately one result of contemporary biblical scholarship in which it is clear that the Hebrew people came rather late to the understanding of the meaning of creation as the act of God. It was through their experience of deliverance from slavery, and through the attempt to live within the covenant established by God with his people that belief in God as the One Lord and Creator of the world came to its full expression. Put in terms of our experience, this means that we speak of God as Creator out of our encounter with his creative power expressed not only in nature but also in his action which gives meaning to our life and history, and supremely in Jesus Christ. We know God as Creator through finding his creative and redemptive power working in our midst.

Therefore when we say God "calls the worlds into being," we are using language that implies the full Christian faith about God as the ultimate source of all things. He is not a vague and mechanical First Cause, or an abstract principle of being, or sheer arbitrary power. God's creation of the world is an action that finds its meaning in the history of his dealing with his creatures. It is from his deeds that we learn who he is.

Who is God? With what language can we speak about him? Our words and symbols are finite. We acknowledge our limitations. But there are words we can use. The Statement uses three phrases:

First, God is Eternal Spirit. When we speak about God's being, we use the word spirit because it brings together the ultimate mystery and the personal reality of God. "God is spirit," thus the Bible speaks about him. In this way it links God's being with ours, for man also is spirit. When the Bible speaks of man as spirit, it means the full personal reality of human existence. It does not mean a substance added to a body, but the living, personal power of responsible and creative life. Spirit, as the Bible speaks of it, is never a purely objective "thing." It is the moving, feeling, loving, free power of personal existence. Of course spirit may become distorted and destructive. There are "evil spirits." But spirit is always the inner dynamic and quickening power at work in existence. To say that God is spirit then is to acknowledge God as living, personal, creative life. At the same time it is to acknowledge the limits of our knowledge, for spirit is mystery, and in the depth of God's being it has its only true definition. We have then a language for speaking about God, although we acknowledge its symbolic character.

God is eternal. God alone is everlasting. He does not come into being or pass away. He is the source of all passage, all becoming. But his is the eternity of creative spirit. He is not aloof from time and change. He acts. The Statement does not further elaborate the interpretation of God's nature. There are endless questions we can ask about God, his relation to time and change, his power and the freedom of his creatures, his knowledge, his presence in and through all things, and his transcendence. These are all themes for Christian reflection, which are related to God's being as eternal spirit. The Statement of Faith gives the essential affirmation about God and sets us out on the road of further interpretation in company with all Christian thought about God through the ages.

Second, the Statement speaks of God as "Father of our Lord Jesus Christ." The fully personal term in the Bible for God is Father. It is possible for us to speak in this way because in Jesus Christ we have seen the love of Father and Son given its full expression in a personal life. Of course from the human point of view we are using an analogy drawn from the human family in order to speak about God. There are other analogies in the Bible such as the husband-wife relationship which is applied to the relation between God and Israel. But in the Christian faith the personal meaning of all such ways of speaking is given to us in the trust, obedience, and communion with God which we see in the sonship of Jesus. Hence the meaning of our personal language about God receives its clarification in the way in which God has become a person for us in Jesus Christ.

"And our Father." Jesus taught the disciples to pray, "Our Father." The New Testament affirms the unique relationship of Jesus to God, but it also speaks of sonship to God as the true fulfillment of every life. Jesus is the Son of God in the special sense that he is God's own word to mankind. He is, as the Fourth Gospel says, the "only begotten Son." But God has revealed in Christ his intention that all should know themselves as his sons. "For all who are led by the Spirit of God are sons of God" (Rom. 8:14). "In Christ Jesus you are all sons of God, through faith" (Gal. 3:26). God has opened up for us the meaning of sonship through Jesus Christ.

We have here then the Christian affirmation of the personal and loving relationship with God and one another which God intends for all. We are children of one Father. It has been the fashion in some criticisms of liberal theology to say that the New Testament does not teach "the fatherhood of God and the brotherhood of man" as general ideals. It is true these may become abstract and ineffective generalities if we separate the meaning of fatherhood and sonship from the revelation in Jesus Christ.

The full meaning of God's fatherhood and human brotherhood are not derived from general human experience, but in the Christian faith the standard of sonship is given in the history of man's relationship to God which culminates in Jesus' supreme demonstration of sonship. So also the brotherhood of man is not to be understood merely as an idealistic concept based on a universal human intuition. There may be worthy elements in such a conception, but the Christian faith points to the concrete fellowship which God has created in human history through his judgment and his mercy. "As you did it to one of the least of these my brethren, you did it to me," says Jesus (Matt. 25:40). The intent and scope of the assertion of the "fatherhood of God and the brotherhood of man" ought not to be disparaged. It has its real roots in the biblical faith that God makes all men one in the community of life and that we find our brother in every child of God, even "the least."

*The Trinity*. The Statement of Faith may seem to have passed by the explicit doctrine of the Trinity—God as Father,

Son, and Spirit, three persons united in one Deity. Is this distinctively Christian formulation of the doctrine of God left out of the Statement of Faith?

What the Statement really does is to use all the necessary terms in which the New Testament speaks of God as Father, Son, and Spirit without explicitly relating these in the formal pattern of a Trinitarian doctrine. It may be remarked, with Martin Luther, that this is what the New Testament itself does. It speaks of the Father, and of the Son who was "with God" and "was God," and of the Spirit, but it does not give us a formal doctrine of the Trinity. That developed only through centuries of the church's reflection and discussion.

The Statement of Faith therefore does not in any way reject the significance of the doctrine of the Trinity. It goes back to those assertions about God which grow out of the revelation of Jesus Christ as his Son, and which gave rise to the later doctrinal formulation. There are good reasons for keeping this freedom from any one Trinitarian formula. There have been many versions of the meaning of the Trinity and the question needs to be handled with the greatest care lest it become a kind of theological word game. Augustine found profound meaning in the doctrine and wrote superbly about it, but his advice is pastoral and practical as he says: "In our inquiry concerning the Trinity and our knowledge of God, the first thing for us to learn is the nature of true love—or rather the nature of love, for only the love which is true deserves the name."[1]

The vital truths guarded by the doctrine of the Trinity are acknowledged in the Statement of Faith. One of these is that the one God has life, power, and action in his own being. He *begets* his Son and *expresses* his Spirit. God is not a static, uncreative being. God is living, personal freedom and he expresses his freedom in the fullness of his creative life. The

[1] Augustine, *On the Trinity*, VIII, 9 (vi).

Statement of Faith makes this conception of God its fundamental affirmation.

Again, the doctrine of the Trinity expresses the social
dimension of God's nature. The conception of Father and Son
bound together by the Spirit of love is one way of expressing
the full meaning of the New Testament statement "God is
love." Augustine found this a favorite way of explicating the
Trinity. It is not the number three, but the social and com-
munal nature of love that is important for the meaning of the
Trinity. What the doctrine asserts in no way qualifies the unity
of God. There is one God, the Creator of all things. In his
freedom and love he discloses himself to us through his Son
and his Spirit. So the pattern of all significant community in
some way reflects the majesty of God's love.

Thus the Statement of Faith says what needs to be said
concerning the unity of God's life as expressed through his
love for his Son. Christians must try to say as clearly as possible how they speak of God so as to acknowledge the depth
and richness of his self-revelation. It is that acknowledgment
which marks the Trinitarian spirit, and it is that spirit which
the Statement of Faith expresses without making a more specific doctrinal formulation.

# He Calls
# and Creates

*He calls the worlds into being,*
*creates man in his own image*
*and sets before him the ways of life and death.*

"Calls" here is a way of saying "creates," and the word
"creates" itself appears in the next phrase concerning man.
Why "calls"? The answer is that this is the essential biblical
interpretation of the meaning of creation. God creates through

his word. Creation is the personal and spiritual act of divine power. It is not a mechanical or physical process, but the act of bringing into being what otherwise lies in nothingness. According to the great creation story of Genesis 1, "God said, 'Let there be light'; and there was light." Through the whole account there runs the theme of God's "calling" his world into being. This is echoed in Psalm 33:6:

> By the word of the Lord the heavens were made,
> and all their host by the breath of his mouth.

And in Hebrews 11:3:

> By faith we understand that the world was created
> by the word of God.

Two points are of special importance in this view of creation:

First, the Statement does not try to give an explanation of the processes of creation. It declares that creation has its source in the will and purpose of God alone. Speculation about the mode of creation or about the beginning of time and its end would be out of place here. The natural history of the world is a matter for the continuing exploration of science. Modern science has given us an evolutionary picture of the universe, indeed of innumerable universes, existing through unimaginable billions of years. One interesting aspect of the Statement of Faith is that it speaks of "worlds" in the plural. This obviously reflects our intellectual situation in the twentieth century. The old picture of the cosmos as a three-layered structure with the earth in the center, heaven above, and hell beneath is not the modern picture of the universe. There are millions of galaxies like ours. The vastness of the cosmos stretches beyond our imagination. The biblical faith in the Creator sets us free for an unending inquiry into this great mystery because it affirms that at the heart of it there is one life-giving, form-creating reality, the creative purpose of God. Whatever worlds there may be, they depend upon the one divine power and order.

The second aspect of the meaning of God's "calling" the worlds into being is that this relates the meaning of creation to the faith that Christ, the Word of God, is present in all creation. The Fourth Gospel speaks of the Logos, the Word, as being from the beginning with God and says that "without him was not anything made that was made." It was this Word which became flesh and dwelt among us. Thus God creates by the same word that became his incarnate saving power, his grace and truth manifest in Jesus Christ. The implication is that we see more fully into the meaning of God's calling the worlds into being when we understand the creation in the light of Christ.

Certainly God's creative power is manifest in all that he has made:

> The heavens are telling the glory
> of God;
> and the firmament proclaims his
> handiwork.
> —Psalm 19:1

Paul says that God's eternal power and deity have been manifest from the beginning in what he has made (Romans 1:20). The Statement in no way denies knowledge of God outside the Christian revelation, but it says that knowledge of who the Creator is and what he intends for his world is unfolded in the course of history, and that it reaches its climax in the truth disclosed in Christ. God calls the worlds into being, and in Christ he calls us to be his new creation (2 Corinthians 5:17).

The word almighty, which the ancient creeds use in speaking of God, is omitted from the Statement of Faith. If the omission is deliberate, it is, perhaps, because the Christian conscience has become increasingly restive under the view that asserts God's omnipotence in such a way that God is held to be the cause of everything that happens. This view has always cast serious doubt on the possibility of human freedom. Further, the traditional interpretation of "almightiness" led to some questionable consequences regarding God's relationship to evil. If he causes everything, it is hard to see how he can be relieved of responsibility for evil.

All theology has the problem of evil to face, and there is no satisfactory answer as to why it should be present in God's universe. Many Christians however have been willing to take the view that the possibility of evil is the price of freedom, and that God has all the power which he can have and still remain a loving God who wills real freedom for his creatures. We need not think of God as the sole cause of everything that happens; we can say "God does not will everything that happens, but he wills something in everything that happens."[2] Those who would hold to more traditional formulations of God's omnipotence have been careful to insist in recent times that human freedom must still be affirmed even if it lands theology in insoluble paradoxes.

The Statement of Faith does not take sides on this question; but, it may be fairly said, it puts its emphasis on the view that God gives his creatures a measure of freedom. The very word "calling" as a synonym for creation suggests that God in his sovereignty gives real responsibility to his creatures. He binds them to himself not with sheer omnipotent force but in the relationship of a free and loving response. This interpretation of the Statement is reinforced by the assertions about the creation of man.

*He creates man in his own image.* The Statement makes man's bearing the image of God an affirmation of faith. This says something both about God and about man. It declares that

[2] This formulation has been attributed to Emil Brunner.

there is a holy and indispensable bond between God and man. The term "image of God" comes from the biblical account of creation. Three times in Genesis it is affirmed that God has created man in his image (Genesis 1:26; 1:27; 5:1). The divine injunction against taking another human life is connected with man's bearing of the image of God, set forth in Genesis 9:6. The psalmist declares that God has made man but "little less than God" (Ps. 8:5).

This is the biblical way of asserting the dignity and responsibility of man as God's creature, endowed with capacities for creativity, love, and freedom. The term image may suggest a mirror, something passive, but in the biblical sense it means the active personal relationship that God establishes as the very foundation of man's existence.

The precise meaning to be attached to the "image of God" has indeed been the subject of much discussion through the centuries. This is partly because of the brief and cryptic use of the term in Genesis, partly because Genesis uses two Hebrew words in close parallelism for "image," and partly because the discussion of the image has been bound up with the question of what happens to original human nature as a result of sin. It is clear that the Bible knows nothing of a "lost" image of God. Even in his sin, man remains one who bears the marks of his divine origin and his responsibility to God. At the same time, sin distorts this relationship, and it mars the real humanity that God intends.

Most Christian theology has spoken of the image of God as being defaced and at least partially lost, in the fall. The Protestant Reformers, particularly Luther and Calvin, used even more radical language; they spoke of the image as lying in "ruins," as being almost totally lost. Yet even they did not make the loss absolute, for they wanted to assert that even in his sin man finds his origin in God reflected in his spirit, his reason, and his creative power.

Interpretations of the image of God in twentieth-century Christian thought have emphasized that it is not a static form but the dynamic relationship between conscious, free responsible man and his Creator. In the Genesis account the most obvious interpretation of the image is man's "dominion" over nature, and over the animals. It points to his special place of creative mastery within the world. Christian thought has always assigned a special place to the dignity of man's reason, his creativity, his high human powers in speaking about the image of God.

Following a suggestion of Dietrich Bonhoeffer's, Karl Barth has developed the view that the image of God is connected in the Genesis account with man's creation as "male and female." This means that the image of God is reflected not in individual capacities or powers alone but in human relationships. It is our creation in community, as persons made to live with one another in mutual support and communion that we find the reflection of God's being.[3]

There are exegetical questions here that still occupy the attention of biblical scholars. Some see in the image a more general assertion concerning man's responsibility to God and his neighbor rather than a specific reference to the sexual form of human life. We need not pursue here the issues in this interpretation. The Statement of Faith connects its assertion of God as creator of all worlds, with the faith that man is called to a special place in the creation. Man has the high dignity of being able to hear the Word of God, and to respond to it, and he has the spiritual capacity to use and to misuse his freedom. Man who bears the image of God is therefore not merely an object to be categorized among other objects in the world, but he is the center of the history of God's dealing with his responsible creatures.

[3] Karl Barth, *Church Dogmatics* (Edinburgh: T. & T. Clark, 1960), Vol. III/I, sec. 45.

This affirmation sets forth the basis for a true Christian humanism. Christianity sets the highest possible worth upon every human life. The human face, even when distorted in anger or fear, is still the face of the man who is intended to know God and his neighbor in love and respect. The great works of human culture—science, art, politics—shot through as they are with human weakness and tragedy, are yet precious in the sight of God who has called man to a kind of partnership in creation. It is through this biblical faith that man has come to the high sense of his power to make history and to remake his environment.

From this point of view the work of the world is part of the good creation, and man's responsibility is to participate in that work. Everything genuinely human that leads to mutual concern, mutual delight, and hopeful human effort to bring meaning into life finds approval and encouragement in the Christian faith. A genuine humanism in this sense belongs in the Christian view of life.

When we consider the image of God from the New Testament point of view we see how the meaning of Jesus Christ involves the final disclosure and transformation of the biblical theme. In the New Testament it is Jesus Christ who is "the likeness of God" (2 Cor. 4:4). The New Testament sees God's redemptive work as the transformation of man into the fullness of the divine image as Christ has revealed that image: "We all, with unveiled face, beholding the glory of the Lord, are being changed into his likeness from one degree of glory to another" (2 Cor. 3:18). Here then is further reason for conceiving the image of God as a dynamic relationship rather than a static order. The image of God is not only the structure of our past and present, but it is the form of our destiny. Man is the unfinished creation, and the Christian hope is that every child of God will be transformed into the likeness of Christ, the true image of God.

*God sets before man the ways of life and death.* The biblical creation story tells not only of something done, but of something begun. In the narratives in Genesis, Adam and Eve represent man in his primordial created state. They are given the garden to tend, but also a warning concerning their obedience to the Creator. They are forbidden to eat of the tree of knowledge of good and evil. But they are tempted and do eat, and the story of man as sinner is begun.

We do not need to be preoccupied with the elements of the story that reflect some early mythological ideas, such as that which makes the taboo on knowledge the crux of the issue of obedience to God. There may be here in the story the insight that man realizes good and evil as concrete possibilities only after he has turned away from God and sought to make himself the law of his life. Thus the story signifies man's loss of integrity and the beginning of his contention with God from whom he is estranged, and the key to the biblical view of history is disclosed. Man is created to enter into a responsible, trusting companionship with God. There are put before him conditions of abundant life on God's terms. Man is tempted to turn away from God. So in the story of creation there is the theme of the divine offer of life with conditions, and man's having to choose between obedience and estrangement from God.

The creation story presents in universal terms the form of the special covenant that God establishes with the Hebrew people after their deliverance from slavery in Egypt. In the faith of Israel God makes himself known to this people as the God who demands their absolute loyalty, and who will fulfill their hopes on the terms which he sets. In the Deuteronomic account of the giving of the law, these words are spoken in the name of God:

> "See, I have set before you this day life and good, death and evil. If you obey the commandments of the Lord your

God which I command you this day, by loving the Lord your God, by walking in his ways, and by keeping his commandments and his statutes and his ordinances, then you shall live and multiply, and the Lord your God will bless you in the land which you are entering to take possession of it. But if your heart turns away, and you will not hear, but are drawn away and worship other gods and serve them, I declare to you this day, that you shall perish; you shall not live long in the land which you are going over the Jordan to enter and possess."

—Deuteronomy 30:15–18

Thus does Israel set out upon its new history as the people of God. This remarkable passage stands in the background of the whole biblical interpretation of history. Man is given a supreme opportunity to realize his life in its wholeness as the servant of a righteous God; but man has freedom to turn to the way which leads to death. So Jeremiah hears the word of God: "And to this people you shall say: 'Thus says the Lord: Behold, I set before you the way of life and the way of death'" (Jer. 21:8).

But what kind of life, and what kind of death? For the most part the Old Testament perspective is focused upon this present life and this history. It is concerned with concrete fulfillment of the hopes of these people for a secure, free, glorious existence in the promised land as the essential meaning of life. Death means loss of this hope. It is to be cut off from such a fulfillment of the national life.

As the people of the Old Testament go on through their tragic experiences the question about the nature of life and death becomes more complex. For one thing the Old Testament is little concerned with thought about life after death. At best it is a shadowy existence and has no positive meaning as a realm of fulfillment. It is the destiny of the nation that counts. But as the trials and tragedies of the national history continue, hope turns more and more to a new order which God himself will establish. Yet the form of the promise and choice remains, a life as the people of God or the death of being cut off from God.

The words "life and death" here are symbols for the two possibilities that God puts before man, but the concrete content of these symbols grows and alters in the course of human experience, and through God's continuing revelation. Physical life and death either for the individual or the nation become less important, and the spiritual reality of life abundant as children of God and death a fruitless existence without him become more clearly the meaning of the choice that lies before man.

What is striking about the Statement of Faith is that it leaves these stark symbols of life and death standing opposed to one another as these are set before man by God. This is an affirmation of the freedom that God gives to man in history.

There are real choices and decisions. There is both warning and promise in the covenant between God and man. As history goes on man discovers that life and death are strangely mixed and that both must be reconceived before their full import can be understood, yet this radical freedom for man before God remains at the heart of the Christian view of history.

## He Seeks
## to Save

*He seeks in holy love to save all people*
*from aimlessness and sin.*

The ways of life and death have been set before man, and he chooses the ways that lead to death. If this is too stark a way of putting the matter, at least it can be said that man has fallen into confusion about which ways lead to real life. Man has turned away from his right relationship to God. Therefore the deeds of God are directed toward dealing with man as he actually is. The Statement describes this situation with two words, aimlessness and sin.

*Sin.* Sin is that wrongness in life for which we men are responsible. Sin is personal estrangement from God and our neighbor. It is the corruption of the image of God. At the same time it could not exist without that image, for only a responsible being who knows something of his true obligation can sin. The Statement does not enter into an explanation of sin or a description of how it came into the world. It simply says that we are sinners. It implies that all men are involved in sin and its consequences; but it does not commit us to the view that there is nothing sound and constructive left in human nature after it is deformed by sin.

This "universality" of sin raises important issues in the Christian view of man. In traditional Christian thought, resting in part upon a literal interpretation of the story of Adam and Eve, the doctrine of "original sin" was taken as the explanation of our universal human plight. On the basis of the view that all men inherit or participate in the sin of Adam, it was declared that each person is born into the world bearing the corruption of original sin. This doctrine served as an "explanation" of the manifestation of sin throughout human life. But it always led to a protest from those who desired to stress the potential goodness of man as well as his inclination to evil. Some interpretations of original sin offended the sense of justice by assigning to every child born into the world a corruption for which he is held responsible but about which he can do nothing.

We can recognize the truth in the doctrine of original sin without tracing the human condition back to one act of the first man. The truth is that we are members one of another in this human family; and when sin has entered, it becomes the status of all. We are born into a world where we share the moral burden of a history of mutual wrong, of destructiveness, of our making idols of clan and nation, a world of radical injustices and the corrupting passions of revenge and greed. This may be called the "objective status" of man as sinner. To exist in this world is to share that condition. At the same time we have individually and collectively a measure of freedom. The way we respond to this world and its orders and possibilities is determined both by what we take in from our social inheritance and by our acts of freedom and decision. To speak of sin is to speak confessionally, each person for himself, and each community for itself. The belief in the universality of sin is not a prediction as to what men will do, but a confession as to what all men actually do with their freedom.

The Statement here speaks of *sin* in the singular, later of *sins* in the plural. Both meanings are necessary; but the discussion of sin as status leads to a point concerning the nature of sin which must not be overlooked. "Sins" in the plural refer to specific acts that are wrong in the sight of God and offenses against our neighbor. Lying, selfishness, murder, adultery, indifference to the suffering of others, self-righteous hypocrisy. These are sins. The list can be multiplied endlessly. The seven deadly sins in the catalog of medieval theology were pride, envy, anger, sloth (acedia), avarice, gluttony, and lust. These are transgressions of specific requirement of God's love and his law.

There is, however, something more in our sinning than specific acts of wrongdoing. Sin has its roots in the depths of human freedom. We men turn away from an ordered and trusting relationship to God and seek to make ourselves the center of meaning in the universe. It is the underlying source of sin which now needs to be identified. Transgressions of the divine law are sins indeed, but the specific acts are symptomatic of a corruption in the soul. Unless we recognize that inward rupture of our right relationship to God we become superficial legalists in our approach to sin. We misunderstand the real nature of the sin from which we need to be redeemed. To save us, God must restore us to our "rightful minds."

*Aimlessness.* "Aimlessness" is one of the unusual words in the Statement of Faith which speaks not of sin alone but of *aimlessness* and sin. Why is this word here, and what does it add to the Christian understanding of what we need to be saved from?

It is significant that in the original discussion of the Statement much attention was given to this word, and there was a general insistence that it be retained. This indicates that "aimlessness" says something about how contemporary man experiences his world and his life. The word sin, like all the great words, gets worn smooth by usage. For some it has come to represent a narrow and legalistic understanding of human life. Many today would say that they do not experience guilt for sin as sharply as they experience an emptiness in life, a lack of purpose, an uncertainty as to what it is all about, an aimlessness.

This experience of having no meaning for living is very common in our world in spite of the vast possibilities in modern culture for human expression and enjoyment, and in spite of the great human causes that ought to challenge us. It is the emptiness of the unfocused life. It is the despair over not finding a worthwhile cause that makes life worth the living. However it is experienced, this aimlessness or emptiness is a kind of lostness. What the Statement of Faith recognizes is that there is more than one way of being "lost"; that is, of being estranged from God and our neighbor and from ourselves. The word aimlessness serves well in giving point to this side of our human need.

Such aimlessness may not be cured simply by finding some specific purpose in life. We can have many purposes that do not fill our real need: making money, acquiring prestige, asserting our power over others. There can be self-centered goals. But there is an ultimate aimlessness, a futility and non-direction of life itself which leaves us empty and disheartened. Such aimlessness is a corruption of personality. It leaves a dangerous vacuum which may be filled with demonic passion and self-destructiveness. Critical observers of the history of Germany between the world wars commented on the "vacuum of meaninglessness" that characterized life for many, especially young people. Such a vacuum may be filled by the passions and fury of tribalism and cruelty. No culture or nation is exempt from it. We need to be saved from aimlessness.

Of course there is aimlessness in our sin and sin in our aimlessness. These two aspects of human lostness are not entirely separate, indeed we misunderstand them if we think they are. In our sin we turn away from God and from the cause of building a just and decent order among men. Then we find life loses its direction. So sin creates aimlessness. Aimlessness in turn is the condition into which the sins of self-destructiveness or self-glorification can enter. The Statement of Faith here intends in a concise way to point to the real depth and scope of the human problem. It is worth noticing that it does not say we need to be saved from suffering or trouble or labor, or any of the risks of finite existence. These are all conditions of life to be accepted. God does not promise a life of comfort and ease with all the kinds of security that we naturally crave. No human good need be disparaged, but "a man's life does not consist in the abundance of the things which he possesses: it consists in the worth of the one thing that possesses him"—as Prof. John Knox has written.[4]

*The root of sin.* Sin is the willful disruption of the relationship to God in which alone we can become whole and loyal

[4] John Knox, "Christianity and the Christian," in *The Christian Answer*, ed. Henry P. Van Dusen (New York: Charles Scribner's Sons, 1945).

persons. It is the inward turning of the self away from its rightful direction. It is the denial of the love and justice that ought to bind us to God and our neighbor. There have been three principal ways in which this wrong turning in the self, this core of sin, has been described. The first is unbelief, or lack of trust; the second is pride, in the sense of making ourselves the center of the meaning of life; and the third is concupiscence, which is the self's turning in upon itself and feeding its own desires.

The Protestant Reformers traced the root of sin to what they called "unbelief." They did not mean by this the rejection of certain doctrines, but the refusal to trust God. With their fully personal understanding of the relationship of man and God, the Reformers found the root of sin in man's refusal to accept life on the terms on which God gives it. Each person knows that he is not the center of existence; but all of us are anxious for ourselves, and so we refuse to entrust our lives wholly to the care of him who is the creator and judge of all things. We want security on our own terms. Paul's description of sin in Romans 1 can be understood in this way, as he speaks of wicked men:

> For although they knew God they did not honor him as God or give thanks to him, but they became futile in their thinking and their senseless minds were darkened. Claiming to be wise, they became fools, and exchanged the glory of the immortal God for images resembling mortal man or birds or animals or reptiles.
>
> —Romans 1:21–23

Paul here traces idolatry and self-degradation to dishonesty in the heart of the person. We know that we depend upon God who has called us into life, yet we turn away from him and try to construct gods more satisfying to our cravings. Thus sin as unbelief is disloyalty to the real source and judge of our being.

When we speak of pride as sin, we do not mean the pride of self-respect or taking satisfaction from accomplishing something well. There is indeed a rightful pride in human life. The sin of "pride" means asserting divine superiority for ourselves and our group. The Greek word *hybris* expresses this more precisely than our English word pride. It means man's infinite longing to be as God, to assume full power over his existence, to assert his perfection. One of the most searching interpretations of sin as pride in this sense is found in Reinhold Niebuhr's *Nature and Destiny of Man*[5] in which he discusses its four major forms: pride of intellect, of power, of morality, and lastly, spiritual pride, which is a summation of all the others and which often finds its most effective vehicle in religion because religion has the symbols and the prestige of holiness. Dr. Niebuhr illuminates our understanding of sin in his analysis of the collective dimensions of pride. We make our race, our nation, our cultural values the standard for judging all others. We usually estimate our virtue by our high ideals, rather than by our actual practice. World history is filled with the record of collective pride, feeding upon the power and greatness of nations and civilizations, and leading to a false assertion of the absoluteness of the righteousness of some over against the inferiority of others. We can understand the depth and destructiveness of collective human behavior only by giving full weight to this spiritual corruption. Our wrestle with sin is all the more difficult because we must make value judgments, and we do rightfully contend for the truth as we see it. We recall that in the message of the Hebrew prophets God's judgment falls not alone upon individuals but upon nations and upon classes such as priests, the powerful, and exploiters of the poor. Jesus expresses this judgment upon collective sin when he denounces the "disloyal generation" and weeps over the city of Jerusalem. When we try to understand the meaning of the moral evils in our society, the horror of Auschwitz, the complacency of the comfortable in great cities where millions live

[5] Reinhold Niebuhr, *The Nature and Destiny of Man* (New York: Charles Scribner's Sons, 1941), Vol. I, chap. 7.

in intolerable poverty, we cannot find the cause in the sins of individuals alone. We are sharers in great wrongs.

Sin as concupiscence means that the self turns in upon itself and tries to make its own gratification the center of life. This may take the form of sensual indulgence and escape from responsibility. It may be a step toward self-destruction as the self finds less and less meaning in living because it finds no meaning beyond its own satisfaction. As John Oman said, "Sin is the attempt to get out of life what God has not put into it."[6]

Sin is a violation of the order and law of God, but this violation stems from a failure to use our freedom in love. All sin represents at some point our refusal to entrust our lives to God in a personal, loving, hopeful affirmation that we belong to one community of life with God and our neighbor. Sin is self-isolation, the will to be separate, and thus to remain untouched by the needs of others and by our own need for honest outgoing love.

One further point is necessary here. The Christian life begins with forgiveness and is intended to grow in love and grace; but sin does not disappear. Indeed, we recognize that there are special temptations which come to those who live close to the beauty and power of sacred things. Claims to perfection in the Christian life are always dangerous and often ludicrous. The greatest saints have the humility that comes from their continual sensitivity to the reality of sin. So the church keeps the confession of sin and the sacrament of forgiveness at the center in its service of worship. The church and the churches must confess the sins of pride and lovelessness. In ecumenical conferences it is often in the service of common confession of the sin present in our divisiveness that we begin to find our authentic unity with one another.

[6] John Oman, *Grace and Personality*, first published 1917 (New York: Association Press, 1961), p. 186.

*God's holy love.* The Christian confession of sin should never be an act of despair, for the good news of the gospel is that sin does not have the last word. Our sin is covered by what God himself has done and will do. Here we return to the first part of the sentence we are considering. We have spoken of aimlessness and sin, but the Statement of Faith actually begins on this very point with God and his love: "He seeks in holy love to save all people."

Thus the Statement puts the love of God at the center of its affirmation concerning his redemptive purpose. It is a fair judgment that the formal creeds of the tradition have had far too little to say of the love of God. In the Statement, love is declared to be the foundation of God's deeds. Even before we know ourselves as sinners, God is seeking us. This is indeed the right order and the great truth of the gospel.

Why *holy* love? Is it not enough to say, as the scripture does, that God is love? Here again we have to remember what happens to the great words when they are carelessly used. *Love* is the one English word we have to cover a great variety of experience and relationships. Indeed we may believe, and we have scriptural warrant for doing so, that something of God's love is reflected in all human love. We remember the parable of the prodigal son, and the biblical image of husband and bride for the relation of God and his people. But the word love can be so generalized and sentimentalized that it loses any distinctive character when we speak of the love of God. The message of the Bible is that the love of God has a depth and meaning which we learn from God's giving himself to us in Christ. The New Testament word most often used for God's love, agape, was a commonly used Greek word, and it is sometimes used even in the New Testament for kinds of human love, but it took on a new aspect through its identification with the love God has shown in Christ. Agape is the suffering, forgiving love of God poured out for sinners. In its expression in the Christian life, it can never be reduced to a kind of emotion or human desire. It is the love that is informed by the spirit of Jesus.

> Love is patient and kind; love is not jealous or boastful; it is not arrogant or rude. Love does not insist on its own way; it is not irritable or resentful; it does not rejoice at wrong, but rejoices in the right. Love bears all things, believes all things, hopes all things, endures all things.
>
> —1 Corinthians 13:4–7

When, therefore, the Statement uses *holy* as a qualifier of love, it is affirming the meaning of agape as the love that God has given to us. It is that love which judges all things, which bears the burden of sin, and which finds the way to healing and reconciliation.

"He seeks to save all people." An early draft of the Statement read "to save *his* people." A case can be made for the earlier version. *All* so easily becomes an impersonal abstraction when we talk glibly about "loving all mankind." It is in loving this person here before us, this neighbor in our street, the man who opposes us, the one in need who can give nothing in return, that we learn what love in the New Testament sense really is. To say God loves *his* people is to stress the concreteness of the divine action. He does not love us because we are examples of an abstract ideal. He loves his own people, his creatures as they are and where they are.

But the final version of the Statement changes "his people" to "all people" in order to avoid one possible misunderstanding that has plagued Christian thought for nearly twenty centuries. When men have thought of God's power as more fundamental than his love, they have sometimes taken the view that since God could save all, then if any are lost it must be because God wills it. There have even been doctrinal formulations that said God predestines some to be lost and spend eternity in hell.

The Christian conscience has protested against such grim and loveless teaching, and it is characteristic of the tendency of most Christian thought in these last centuries to have moved away from it. The Universalist Christian communion arose as a protest against the view that God will allow any to be lost. The Statement neither affirms nor denies the universalist view that all will ultimately be saved, but it does make a clear and unmistakable affirmation that God's loving intention embraces the fulfillment and reconciliation of every one of his creatures.

To affirm that God seeks to save all is to say something more than that he includes each one within his loving concern. He saves us not only as individuals but all together. Salvation means more than bringing us one by one into a new relationship to God, though that is one side of what happens. Salvation also is the healing and renewing of man in his solidarity. Dietrich Bonhoeffer felt keenly that a stress upon individual salvation alone distorts the message of the gospel which is directed toward the creation of new humanity bound together in one order of life. Concern about one's own salvation can be merely self-centered. Concern about the salvation of mankind with fulfillment in freedom and creative life for all is an authentic expression of love.

The Statement maintains a bulwark against any doctrine that God has a favored people, nation, or race. It brings every human being within the scope and orbit of the divine love. It makes it unmistakably plain that he who professes to live within the love shown us in Christ is to become the servant of every neighbor, regardless of his class, status, creed, or condition in life. The holiness of love implies the wholeness of the one human family under God.

# He
# Judges

*He judges men and nations by his righteous will
declared through prophets and apostles.*

The God who seeks to save must judge. This is not a world in which "anything goes," but a world with conditions set for it which must be met if life is to be fulfilled. The Statement affirms the theme of God's righteous will and identifies the prophets and apostles as those through whom the will of God is declared to men. As a prelude to the affirmation about Jesus Christ, this sentence states the way in which the faith of Israel with its prophetic message becomes the foundation and anticipation of the salvation that God manifests in Jesus Christ. We are concerned here then with the view of history held by the prophets. In the reference to both the apostles and the prophets, the Statement binds Old Testament and New Testament together, for the apostles are witnesses to Jesus Christ. The whole affirmation gives implicit recognition to the witness of scripture as the primary source of our knowledge of the deeds of God.

The question may rightly be asked whether there is here a sufficient recognition of the nature and authority of the Bible. There is more in scripture than prophetic and apostolic witness. There are also histories, liturgies, psalms, wisdom literature. Further, the New Testament writings are not all apostolic in the strict sense of that term, and yet the entire Statement is built upon a scriptural pattern. The prophetic and apostolic witness is the heart of scripture as it points to the acts of God and his saving word in Jesus Christ. We shall see that the prophetic word is not only preserved but emphasized in the New Testament. Allowing then for an economy of words, the

Statement does give us the biblical basis for knowing Jesus Christ as the culmination of the prophetic faith because he embodies in his life and work God's righteousness and the power of his judgment. Thus the Statement sees the themes of God's love, his judgment, and his righteous will binding the whole of biblical history together.

Several aspects of the prophetic message contribute to the meaning of this article.

*The faith of the prophets.* First, "God judges men and nations." In the experience of the Hebrew people, God made himself known through the relationship he established with the nation. He makes a people his people, and creates a covenant relationship with them. Of course this includes God's acts and words disclosed to individuals. There are the great persons in Israel's history—Abraham, Isaac, Jacob, Moses, David, and Solomon. And there are the prophets, such as Elijah, Amos, Isaiah, and Jeremiah. God judges both the individual and the nation. So Isaiah says, "I am a man of unclean lips, and I dwell in the midst of a people of unclean lips" (Isa. 6:5). But the history of the individual is set within the history of God's concern with that whole people called to serve him as their one God and to obey his law.

We recognize that the Old Testament conception of the nation was bound up with the doctrine of election, God's choice of one people to be his witnesses to the world. The Statement does not speak of election, and the whole conception needs to be carefully interpreted in the light of its development in Israel's history. It is clear in the prophetic view that election confers no special privileges upon Israel. The judgment of God falls upon all nations; but, as the prophets continually insist, it falls with special weight upon Israel just because this people has been granted an intimate and special knowledge of God's will.

The theme of God's love and care for the one people becomes the crucial case by which God's action in history is to be understood. The prophets recognize the special responsibility of Israel because Israel has been granted a peculiar knowledge of God, but they know God as the one Lord of all nations and all history who works out his purposes in the sweep of history. The prophets look for a new covenant, a law written on the heart which transcends all national particularity (Jeremiah 31).

The second aspect of prophetic faith is the affirmation that God's judgment is the expression of his "righteous will" for all peoples. God's righteousness is his justice. The Old Testament uses two words for God's justice, *tsedeq* and *mishpat*. They both express the character of God's will. God is righteous in the sense that he sets the conditions for the fulfillment of life as the Creator intends it. His will embraces the whole of life, the relationship of men and nations, their obligations toward one another whether king or servant, kinsman or alien, blood brother or stranger. Hence the righteousness that is God's justice involves concrete obligations for every man and every people. There is a divine law, expressed in the commandments of God. We see clearly why the Hebrew people never thought of religion as one part of life separate from such human activities as politics, buying and selling, international relations, the obligations of strong and weak or of rich and poor, family loyalty and care. God's righteous will embraces the whole of life. Man can serve God only by honoring the demand for justice in every relationship, and God judges the life of the nation by its effect upon every person in the whole society.

The third characteristic of the prophetic faith is the conception of God's judgment as exercised through his specific action in history. He visits the consequences of unrighteousness upon the nations, thus exhibiting his will as the only basis for the fulfillment of man's life on earth. It is true that God's judgment does not mean total rejection of man as he is. God upholds the righteous man; but it is clear that the accent falls for the most part upon the wandering of Israel from the absolute loyalty and obedience that the covenant with God requires. The result is that God visits suffering and disruption upon the nation as righteous judgment against unrighteous men. Jeremiah declares:

> "Thus says the Lord of hosts, the God of Israel: You have seen all the evil that I brought upon Jerusalem and upon all the cities of Judah. Behold, this day they are a desolation, and no one dwells in them, because of the wickedness which they committed."
>
> —Jeremiah 44:2–3

There are great questions raised by this conception of God's judgment which we must ask again in our own time and in the face of the wreckage of war and riot. How far can we say that the failure to find a peaceful and orderly way of life for all the peoples that dwell upon the face of the earth is a moral failure? In what sense can we think of the suffering and destruction in social conflict as a direct expression of the judgment of God? These were questions for the prophets which led them to an agonizing search for the meaning of the judgment of God. But throughout the whole of the prophetic struggle with the meaning of God's sovereignty in history, the fundamental conviction is maintained that there is a divinely willed active righteousness which men must seek and obey, and that there are real consequences in suffering and in the destruction of human hopes and ideals for nations and cultures when they are built upon injustice.

Certainly the question of what constitutes a just order of life becomes of critical importance. Here the prophets make their supreme contribution to our moral understanding. It is the central demands of justice and mercy rather than the forms of religious observance or scrupulosity in petty matters which count ultimately before God.

> For I desire steadfast love and not sacrifice,
>   the knowledge of God, rather than burnt offerings.
>                    —Hosea 6:6

Social justice as the foundation of the right relationship between man and God is the central message of the prophets. In their understanding of justice there was a special concern for the poor and the weak. The prophets never forgot that their people had been slaves in Egypt and had been delivered from oppression. They continually pronounced God's judgment upon those who "trample upon the needy, and bring the poor of the land to an end" (Amos 8:4). In our present day when the effects of crowded and inadequate housing are critical matters in our cities, and where the amount of space we occupy has become a moral issue, we can read Isaiah's condemnation:

> Woe to those who join house to house,
>   who add field to field,
> until there is no more room.
>                    —Isaiah 5:8

Out of the concern to protect the helpless against the powerful, a special insight into the divine righteousness and the divine judgment emerges in Israel's faith. God's judgment is often a reversal of human judgment and expectations. God turns history upside down and upsets the calculations of the powerful. According to the view of Isaiah 10:1-4, "Those who rob the poor and make the fatherless their prey on the day of punishment will have no one to whom to flee for help. They can do nothing but crouch among the prisoners or fall among the slain."

One of the decisive expressions of this revolutionary judgment of God comes in the Magnificat, the hymn of Mary:

"He has shown strength with his arm,
he has scattered the proud in the imagination
of their hearts,
he has put down the mighty from their
thrones,
and exalted those of low degree."
—Luke 1:51–52

We begin to see how questionable are simple predictions concerning the course of God's judgment. The story of Israel is the story of the search for the full understanding of God's way with his people.

As the experience that lies behind our Old Testament continued through the exile of the Hebrews, their return, the misfortunes of their continuing wars against the conquerors who overran Palestine, something happened to the prophetic view of history and the expectation regarding the judgment of God. The question became ever more sharp, "How long does it take before God's will is done in history?" The vindication of the righteous is a hope, but the actualities of history do not exhibit it. Is suffering always a punishment for wrongdoing? This is the question raised in the book of Job, and the answer given there moves beyond the view that there is a simple correlation between righteousness and well-being.

If suffering is not necessarily a punishment for wrongdoing, neither is prosperity necessarily a sign of the virtue of the prosperous or their favor in God's sight. This point might well be remembered in the composing of Thanksgiving Day proclamations. We ought to be grateful for what we have without ascribing to ourselves superior righteousness; but that is a level of insight that requires humility, prayer, and repentance, especially among the powerful and affluent. The prophets saw quite clearly that in a worldly sense the wicked may prosper. This too makes the discernment of the meaning of God's justice a subtle and difficult problem.

As the contrast between God's holiness and man's sin is sharpened, the radical question is asked by the prophets: "Are there any who are righteous in the sight of God?" Perhaps there will be only a remnant of the nation to preserve faith and loyalty. Suppose even the remnant disappears. What will God do with a history in which his holy will has been violated?

The sharpening of these questions and the continued suffering of the nation lies behind the messianic hope that God will do a new thing in history. He will reestablish the nation and a righteous order of life through one who will execute his judgment and display the divine power.

> There shall come forth a shoot
>> from the stump of Jesse,
>> and a branch shall grow out of
>> his roots.
> And the Spirit of the Lord shall
>> rest upon him,
>> the spirit of wisdom and
>> understanding,
>> the spirit of counsel and might,
>> the spirit of knowledge and the
>> fear of the Lord.
> —Isaiah 11:1–2

The later Isaiah sees in the coming one the vindication of God's justice.

> The Spirit of the Lord God is
>> upon me,
>> because the Lord has anointed me
> to bring good tidings to the
>> afflicted;
>> he has sent me to bind up the
>> brokenhearted,
> to proclaim liberty to the captives,
>> and the opening of the prison to
>> those who are bound;
> to proclaim the year of the Lord's
>> favor.
> —Isaiah 61:1–2

There were many forms of the messianic hope. In the period between the testaments a type of thought flourished that is called "apocalyptic," in which the Messiah begins to be thought of as a supernatural messenger of God who comes not only to establish a new historical order but also to establish a new heaven and a new earth. It is in this mood of intense expectancy concerning a dramatic new act of God which will bring his kingdom into power over all things that the New Testament begins with its message that "the kingdom of God is at hand." The messianic hope was the fruit of the prophetic faith in God's righteous sovereignty over history.

We must add one further theme in this summary of the prophetic faith. It appears in the great poems that constitute the prophecy of the Second Isaiah, which begin at Isaiah 40. In Isaiah 53 a new vision of the Servant of God appears together with a new assertion concerning the way in which God executes his judgment. The Servant of God is the one who bears the afflictions of his people. His vicarious suffering opens the way to the salvation of mankind.

> Surely he has borne our griefs
>   and carried our sorrows;
> yet we esteemed him stricken,
>   smitten by God, and afflicted.
> But he was wounded for our
>     transgressions,
>   he was bruised for our iniquities;
> upon him was the chastisement
>     that made us whole,
>   and with his stripes we are
>     healed.
> —Isaiah 53:4–6

The identification of the Servant in this great passage is still one of the mysteries. Is the Servant an individual, a prophet, or an ideal type created by the poet? Or is the Servant Israel itself? We can see that the conception of a vicarious bearing of the consequences of sin opening the way to the healing and saving of men is here given dramatic expression. The church later used this prophetic word in its interpretation of Jesus' suffering and death. From this starting point, the meaning of discipleship reaches its full power in the conception of the Suffering Servant. (See pages 99–101.)

*The mercy of God.* We conclude this discussion of the prophetic view of judgment with an observation about the relation of judgment and mercy. The overtone of the word judgment usually suggests the execution of punishment for wrong. It connotes the wrath of God against evil, and this idea certainly belongs in any biblical interpretation of judgment. But we remember that God judges "by his righteous will," as the Statement says. This means that the love and mercy in God's righteousness enter into his judgment.

It is true that there is much in the concrete personal language of the Bible in which God's wrath seems to be opposed to his mercy.

> "In overflowing wrath for a moment
> I hid my face from you,
> but with everlasting love I will have
> compassion on you,
> says the Lord, your Redeemer."
> —Isaiah 54:8

Martin Luther's theology was characterized by a profound sense of the tension between wrath and mercy in God's dealing with man. Yet the outcome of the prophetic faith, not only in the New Testament but also in the faith of Israel, is that while we may speak of "wrath" in God, his *righteousness* is not identical with his wrath. His righteousness is his will for the fulfillment of life for his people. It is not opposed to his love, but is the expression of his love. Perhaps it is the prophet Hosea who gives us the most moving expression of the divine love as the true meaning of God's will:

I will not execute my fierce anger,
I will not again destroy Ephraim;
for I am God and not man,
   the Holy One in your midst,
   and I will not come to destroy.
                              —Hosea 11:9

The prophets knew and declared the love of God. In the New Testament it received a further clarification. The way of God's righteousness and the execution of his judgment and the depth of his mercy are now seen in the light of his deed in Jesus Christ.

*Prophets and apostles.* We have given primary attention here to the prophetic witness rather than to the apostolic, because the apostles are witnesses to Jesus Christ and their message is to be interpreted in the christological part of the Statement of Faith. But we have observed that the Statement links the prophetic and apostolic witnesses together, in part to point to the entire scriptural testimony that lies at the foundation of the Christian faith. There are, however, other important reasons for linking the prophetic and apostolic words.

We should note the meaning of "apostleship." This word has some complications in its usage in the New Testament. It had a general meaning that designated a messenger sent on a specific commission. In the Gospels the word is used of those whom Jesus sent out to preach the message of the kingdom, though only in Luke's account does Jesus call them apostles (see Luke 6:13). The word apostle came to be used in the church to refer to the twelve disciples or to the eleven plus Matthias who replaced Judas. But Paul is an apostle, and clearly there are others who preached the gospel in the early Christian community who are so designated. Soon the church restricted the term to the twelve and to Paul. Roman Catholic and some Anglican doctrines of the church have argued for their interpretation of the place of bishops in the apostolic succession through the relation of the "office" of apostle to the "office" of bishop. The Statement does not enter into these debates, which are hardly resolvable on the basis of the text. What we recognize is that the gospel was proclaimed by men who were messengers of the salvation they had experienced and who told the story of Jesus as witnesses to his disclosure of the righteousness and grace of God. An apostolic church is one that continues this witness.

The apostolic witness in the New Testament reaffirms the prophetic word of God's righteousness and his judgment. Jesus' preaching and teaching continue at so many points the tradition of the great prophets of Israel. His message is filled with the demand for righteousness, the judgment of God upon the exploiters of the poor, the condemnation of the self-righteous who pass by on the other side of human need. He sees a day of reckoning for an evil generation and a disloyal nation (Matthew 13). He declares it is not the will of God that one should perish, but there is no escaping his judgment upon those who do not repent and who do not serve the Lord by meeting the needs of the neighbor (Matthew 18:14; 25). The church emphasizes this prophetic role of Jesus when it says that he bears the title and office of Prophet as well as Priest and King. The apostolic preaching therefore remains true to its witness to Christ as it continues the prophetic message of the divine righteousness and the ultimate judgment before which all men and nations stand.

Yet the righteousness of God takes on a new meaning in the New Testament witness and the apostolic preaching, for the final disclosure of that righteousness is now known in God's action in Jesus Christ. It is Christ who makes incarnate the love of God. He has disclosed both the content of the divine will and the ultimate recourse of the divine mercy in dealing with sinful and lost men. We go on at once to speak of God's deed in Jesus.

# In Jesus Christ
# He Has Come

*In Jesus Christ, the man of Nazareth,*
*our crucified and risen Lord,*
*he has come to us*
*and shared our common lot,*
*conquering sin and death*
*and reconciling the world to himself.*

We have confessed God the Father of our Lord Jesus Christ. Now we say who Jesus Christ is, and what God has done in him. We notice a slight alteration in the style at this point. God is again the subject but the sentence begins, "In Jesus Christ . . . he [God] has come to us . . . ." The stylistic change is deliberate, and it is meant to suggest that what follows is not simply one affirmation among the others, but that which gives the center and key to the whole. What has gone before leads up to Jesus Christ. What comes after follows from what God has done in him.

*The man of Nazareth, our crucified and risen Lord.* When we say Jesus is the Christ we acknowledge him as God's messenger of salvation. *Christ* is the Greek word for the Hebrew *Messiah*. We have seen the growth of the expectation that the Messiah would bring the kingdom of God to fulfillment on earth. The New Testament opens in this atmosphere of tense expectancy. History is to receive its final judgment and God's reign is at hand. Mark records that Jesus came into Galilee preaching the gospel of God: "The time is fulfilled, and the kingdom of God is at hand; repent, and believe in the gospel" (Mark 1:15). He declares to the people "the kingdom of God is in the midst of you"; that is, it is at hand in the message and work of Jesus (Luke 17:21). He sends the disciples out to preach this message. All are warned to make ready, to watch and pray. It will be a day of judgment. "Then two men will be in the field; one is taken and one is left" (Matt. 24:40). This expectation of the imminent kingdom shapes much of the thought and language especially of the first three Gospels.

Our Christian confession is that Jesus did come as God's Messiah bringing with him the judgment and power of God's kingdom. But something happens to the conception of messiahship through the life and teaching of Jesus. "The Messiah who came was not the Messiah who was expected," thus Reinhold Niebuhr put the point succinctly. The disciples were taught by Jesus that the Messiah must suffer. In the light of the crucifixion they had to rethink the meaning of his work. It is this reexamination of the way God brings his kingdom in history which characterizes much of the radical rethinking that runs through the Fourth Gospel and Paul's letters. It is this new conception of how God works in history that is expressed in the church's faith in the majesty and humility of the Son of God who comes in weakness, who takes the suffering of the world upon himself, and who wins his victory through a patient and loyal love. It is this meaning of Jesus' messiahship that we must try to grasp.

The confessional Statement puts the tremendous paradox in a few words: "the man of Nazareth, our crucified and risen Lord." The Messiah came as man, a real human being, who lived and died in the same flesh, facing the same temptations, struggling with the same world that is the common lot of all of us.

The phrase "man of Nazareth" identifies Jesus as the real person who lived in Palestine at a certain time in history. The Statement goes on to speak of his crucifixion, and the whole phrase has the same historical force as does the declaration in the ancient creeds: "crucified under Pontius Pilate." He really lived in that time and place and was executed under the authority of the Roman governor.

We need to consider our knowledge of Jesus as a historical person because the question about that knowledge has concerned the church now for over a century and a half, and there is much contemporary discussion about it. Biblical criticism has given us new insight into the way in which the tradition about Jesus was handed on and became our New Testament writings. In the nineteenth century, scholars set out to reconstruct our picture of the historical facts, a great and honest inquiry that was summarized in Albert Schweitzer's book *The Quest of the Historical Jesus*. Since Schweitzer the scholarly quest has gone on; and the question of how far we can get back to a history that is objectively reliable is still very much to the fore.

It is clear why we are concerned about the historical picture of Jesus. It is not that there is any significant case for the view that "Jesus never lived." The real question is whether we can distinguish in the New Testament what represents the growth of tradition, which has therefore added to and given us later interpretations of the actual history. It has become clear that the Gospels give us a synthesis of faith and fact and that we are not in the situation of having biographies of Jesus which have been written as objective historical documents. They tell us about him as he was remembered and as the meaning of his life was grasped in the new faith of the church. One consequence of Jesus' assumption of our humanity was that the story about him was told by men through the growth of traditions and materials which may not be precise history but which reflect the faith of the community that he brought into being.

Christians therefore will have different judgments about the way in which they understand many elements in the biblical witness to Jesus. We are entitled to use our historical critical judgment and to see elements of symbol and legend at points in the record, for God is truth, and the truth of our faith need not fear any facts of history. At the same time we do not need to have detailed knowledge of all the events in Jesus' life. Our faith rests upon the whole meaning and impact of what he did, as that was experienced first by those who were with him, and throughout the centuries by all who experience the grace and power of his life. We know who he was because of the saving power that he communicates to us, and we welcome all historical investigation into the gospel record.

*Our risen Lord.* The man Jesus is our risen Lord. Thus we express our faith that in Jesus, God revealed the depth of his love and the power of his kingdom. Jesus is God's word incarnate and therefore we call him Lord. The word Lord was in common use in Jesus' time as addressed to kings and emperors. It meant a person with the aura and authority of divinity. But in the disciples' preaching about Jesus it meant that he was God's Messiah, the Word of God in whom the redemption of the world has been accomplished. Peter says, "God has made him both Lord and Christ, this Jesus whom you crucified" (Acts 2:36).

The church sensed from the beginning that the statement "Jesus is God" is awkward, and that it hides rather than expresses the full meaning of the incarnation. God has become man for us. The word Lord acknowledges Jesus as God's word to us. Jesus is fully man even as he is the Word of God incarnate. This is what the church's Council of Chalcedon meant by declaring that in Jesus the divine and human natures are inseparably but unconfusedly together.

Our Statement does not give any formula for the incarnation. There are many ways in which Christians have understood how God and man are together in Jesus. What the Statement does is to bring together the essential affirmations that he was real man, and that he is our Lord.

*He has come to us.* We are telling the deeds of God. We see the life and message of Jesus as the human expression of God's action. The New Testament says throughout that Jesus does his work in obedience to and dependence upon God's work. "I seek not my own will but the will of him who sent me" (John 5:30). "My Father is working still, and I am working" (John 5:17). In the account of the baptism at the beginning of his mission Jesus hears the voice of God, "This is my beloved Son, with whom I am well pleased" (Matt. 3:17). And in Luke 23:46, the final word from the cross is, "Father, into thy hands I commit my spirit!"

The meaning of "he came to us" is not only that God is together with man in Jesus, but that Jesus' life as the Servant of God embodies God's search for man. The prophets came to the insight, expressed most profoundly in Hosea (whom Jesus quotes more frequently than any other), that God yearns for his people and seeks to draw them back to himself. In the Christian witness to Jesus we see him coming to seek and to save the lost. He revealed the active, seeking love of God. What Jesus does, he does as the Servant of what God is doing in history. Macleod Campbell put the point with admirable brevity when he said that Jesus revealed the love of God by trusting it.[7]

*Our common lot.* God has broken through to us by showing what his love means in the actual life of one who lived among us sharing our human situation. This is the force of the phrase "our common lot." It means that God's work of redemption was and is carried out in our life as it is. Whatever goes into our experience of life—being born into the world, growing, loving, hungering and thirsting, seeking our vocation, being misunderstood, facing the disappointments and failures which attend our efforts, experiencing the joy and enigma of friend-

[7] Macleod Campbell, *The Nature of the Atonement* (1856 ed.), p. 283.

ship, seeing injustice and tragedy, knowing that we die—all these things are in the story of Jesus. He was tempted in all points as we are. He found men resisting his message of love, and misunderstanding it. Consider, for example, the disciples who wanted to sit at his right hand in the kingdom (Matthew 20:20–28). When he went home to his familiar Galilee, he could do no mighty work there save a few healings (Mark 6:5). It is possible to read the gospel record as showing that Jesus wrestled within his own soul about the full meaning of his mission, perhaps to the very end. He met the opposition of those who resisted his message and feared his power. He encountered the cold calculations of some who wanted to get rid of him, and he felt the passion and fury of a mob. He died condemned as a disturber of the peace, accused of crimes against the state and against religion.

This conception of messiahship as involving a real human experience created a new understanding of God's action in history and his way of redeeming the world. It is the vision of the divine humility of the Son of God, saving the world by entering in love into the depths of the world's life and its tragedy. He who came into the world from the Creator and Lord of all came as a helpless infant, grew to manhood, acted, suffered, and died. When Dietrich Bonhoeffer reflected on the meaning of the incarnation in the last days of his imprisonment before his execution at the order of Hitler, he said:

> God allows himself to be edged out of the world and on to the cross. God is weak and powerless in the world, and that is exactly the way, the only way, in which he can be with us and help us. Matthew 8:17 makes it crystal clear that it is not by his omnipotence that Christ helps us, but by his weakness and suffering . . . only a suffering God can help.[8]

Matthew 8:17 recognizes in Jesus the one prophesied in Isaiah who "took our infirmities and bore our diseases."

---

[8] Dietrich Bonhoeffer, *Letters and Papers from Prison* (New York: Macmillan, 1962), pp. 219–20.

The Statement leaves open the question of how we shall interpret two aspects of the New Testament record, Jesus' sinlessness and the miraculous signs and powers that accompany his life from beginning to end.

The assertion in Hebrews 4:15 that he was "one who in every respect has been tempted as we are, yet without sinning" makes us ask how Jesus does truly share our common lot. Certainly we acknowledge him as the Christ because he lives a life of utter devotion and obedience in the face of the world's temptations. He reveals what our humanity is intended to be, not just what it is. We can say that Jesus discloses the meaning of sinlessness as the life in which communion with God and obedience to him are never surrendered under the world's onslaught.

We recognize however that Jesus never sets himself apart from sinners or from the suffering that sin causes. One of the offenses charged against him was that he ate with publicans and sinners. He identified himself with his people when he went to be baptized by John, for baptism was the sign of repentance in preparation for the kingdom. Once addressed as "Good Teacher," he replied, "Why do you call me good? No one is good but God alone" (Mark 10:18). While he excoriated the proud and the unjust, he pleaded with the whole nation to recognize the kingdom of God and prepare for it. According to the record of Matthew 23:37, he exclaimed as he wept over Jerusalem: "O Jerusalem, Jerusalem, . . . How often would I have gathered your children together . . . and you would not!"

The word from the cross—"Father, forgive them; for they know not what they do"—is a plea for those whose sin has caused his own agony. It is this complete loyalty to men even in their sin which maintains the bond between Jesus and ourselves. Perhaps this is what Paul means by saying of Jesus that God "made him to be sin who knew no sin" (2 Cor. 5:21). He shared our common lot in the world as it is, not as it might ideally be conceived; and this sharing is the supreme identifica-

tion that God in his love has made with us. "For God so loved
the world that he gave his only Son" (John 3:16).

The sharing of our common lot then is not a preliminary
act of God before he redeems the world; it is the very action of
redemption. The early fathers of the church saw this clearly.
That is why they rejected every interpretation of the incarnation that cast doubt upon Jesus' real humanity. They rejected
the docetic heresy which held that Jesus' human appearance
was only appearance, and that he never really became "en-
fleshed" as we are. This heresy reappears in many forms in the
history of the church. It is present whenever Christianity is
presented as a purely "spiritual" religion that has no real concern with material things or with concrete justice in the
world. Jesus dealt with all the needs of men—bodily, mental,
social, and spiritual. He fed them, healed their bodies and their
minds, demanded justice for them, and taught emphatically
that God is concerned about the things that are necessary to
human existence. "Your heavenly Father knows that you need
them all" (Matt. 6:32). True spirituality as Christianity understands it is a loving concern for everything that goes to make
life good and whole. In the incarnation God acted in his good
world, giving ultimate sanctification to the flesh and the spirit.

We can interpret the miraculous aspects of the story of
Jesus without letting go this conviction that God really as-
sumed our human nature. The miracles that attend the story,
those that Jesus himself performs, and the supreme miracle of
the resurrection, are all signs of the divine power working
through him and around him. But as displays of divine power,
they do not require us to deny his humanity. Indeed, the
miracles have their meaning as signs of the kingdom of God,
not simply as exhibitions of the extraordinary. We see that at
the crucial point of Jesus' confrontation with his opposers in
the loneliness and agony of the cross, he calls upon no miracle
to rescue him. He is taunted with the cry, "Let him take him-

self down from the cross." We can have various interpretations of the Gospels on their miraculous side. Different points of view are quite possible here within the Christian faith and in the interpretation of scripture. But whatever we make of the special signs of God's presence in Jesus, we should not let them obscure the great truth that he shared our common lot.

*Conquering sin and death.* In four words the essential matter is stated. In Jesus Christ, God has won and is winning the victory over sin and death. The shout of victory in the Christian faith, its *alleluia*, has its source here. In Jesus' life, death, and resurrection God has reconstituted our human situation, begun a new history, and has shown that nothing can separate us from him. What is the nature of the victory and how is it won?

There have been many ways in which the meaning and the way of Christ's victory have been interpreted. There is the objective side of what God accomplished in history through Jesus' meeting with the forces that seek to destroy him. And there is the subjective side, of how his victory enters into our experience and we become participants in his death and resurrection. It is worth noting that the church never settled upon one orthodox doctrine of the atonement, which is the word used to express the central act of reconciliation. The reason seems clear. We are speaking of the ultimate meaning of our existence and of how God brings us into a new relationship to him. Aimlessness, sin, and death are all met and overcome. It is too much for any "theory" to encompass. We can only try to say, with the church through the ages, and from the standpoint of our own confession, what Jesus Christ does for us.

The language of the Statement is inspired by the theme of Christ as the conqueror of sin and death. The New Testament describes Jesus' life as meeting the onslaughts of temptation, the rebellion of sinners, the anxieties and fears of mankind. And he meets them all with love. He is "Christus Victor."

Bishop Gustaf Aulén of the Church of Sweden has written one of the important books on the meaning of atonement, and he uses this phrase as his title. He believes that this is the original and fundamental way in which the New Testament thinks of the work of God in reconciliation. It is misleading, he says, to think of Jesus' paying a debt to God to open the way for the divine forgiveness. Jesus' struggle and victory are God's own deed. He is reconciling the world to himself.

We find in the New Testament the account of Jesus' victory won in a struggle with everything that threatens man's life as a loving, faithful child of God. Jesus confronts the temptations of Satan and resists them in the name of God. He drives out the demonic powers that invade bodies and minds and produce illness. He finds himself in conflict with established religious forms and piety. He dares to put the claims of man above the claims of religious observance, as in his teaching about the sabbath. He draws upon himself the hatred of loveless men by his teaching of love for every neighbor and justice for every class and group. He experiences the misunderstanding of his own disciples, and the loneliness of being left at the end to face his death at the hands of the established powers and the passions of the people. While we have to speak with the greatest restraint about Jesus' inner experience, there is surely the suggestion in the account of the prayer in the Garden of Gethsemane and in the cry from the cross ("My God, my God, why hast thou forsaken me?") that he experienced the possibility of the failure of his mission. He went into the depths of human experience with an ultimate trust in God's power. In experiential terms we can say that we know Jesus as the one who gave the love of God and the love of neighbor decisive victory by expressing and trusting that love in the face of everything that threatens or denies it.

The victory over death brings us to a side of the story which we can express partly in life here and now and partly as the basis for our ultimate hope. There is a victory over death in the way Jesus accepts and meets death. This is not the stoic victory of sheer courage and endurance no matter what comes. It is the creative use of death as a way through to the work of reconciliation. "Greater love has no man than this, that a man lay down his life for his friends" (John 15:13). Death here means not only physical dying, but the destruction of hope, the loneliness of life estranged from God. Death becomes a symbol of the aimless life, and the threat of futility. Jesus' death was the blasting of the hopes of the disciples for the coming of the kingdom. It is clear then that the primary ground of the Christian faith in Jesus' victory over death was the experience of the resurrection. However we interpret that experience, it was the beginning of the faith that God had shown in Jesus that he, the eternal Creator and Redeemer, is the Lord even over death.

Thus the resurrection faith became the foundation of the Christian hope in which death is no longer to be feared but is accepted in faith that "whether we live or whether we die we are the Lord's" (Rom. 14:8). Paul indeed recognizes a great mystery in the theme of resurrection. Death is the "last enemy" which Christ must conquer (1 Cor. 15). Yet the victory of the grave has already been supplanted by the victory of the risen Christ. And this victory is won over death which has become a symbol of sin. "The sting of death is sin," Paul says (1 Cor. 15:56). Here Paul identifies estrangement from God as the real source of man's fear of death. The life that is burdened by guilt and hopelessness is a kind of living death. Hence Paul speaks of the deliverance that Christ brings from sin and death as the experience of those who are baptized into Christ's death and are raised with him into newness of life (Rom. 6:3-4).

The heart of the whole matter of Christ's victory is the gracious act of God which restores to us in this flesh that full and trusting life with him in which we can believe that nothing can separate us from the love which he gives. God's grace is his love in action, and at the heart of grace there is forgiveness for sin.

God's forgiveness means more than setting aside a penalty for sin. It is not a juridical action, but a personal action. In Jesus, God shows that he bears with us, shares in the suffering that sin causes, and through his mercy creates a new possibility for us to begin to learn the way of love.

Traditional doctrines of atonement rightly stress the suffering of the cross as essential in our understanding of God's forgiveness. The belief that Jesus bears for us what we cannot bear for ourselves, the consequences of our guilt, has always expressed a dimension of God's grace that gives a powerful release from the burdened conscience. It is the experience of finding that we are accepted in spite of being unacceptable, as Paul Tillich has put it.[9] The doctrine of justification by faith, so much stressed by the Protestant Reformers, meant this complete reliance of the Christian upon God's grace alone, with no claims for the adequacy of our righteousness.

The forgiveness of God is costly because it involves his bearing the consequences of sin. But surely he does not withhold his forgiveness until a certain price has been paid. God gives himself to us in Christ, takes our suffering upon himself as the way through to a new relationship for us. Belief that we are offered a new life through what God does for us is not a way of avoiding responsibility for what we are. To take it in this way is to fall into the peril of what Dietrich Bonhoeffer called "cheap grace." Forgiveness is rather the beginning of the life in which we can dare to confess our full responsibility before God and our neighbor because we no longer have to claim or pretend that we always use our freedom rightly.

[9] Paul Tillich, *The Courage to Be* (New Haven: Yale University Press, 1952), p. 164.

The works of the Christian are to be the acts of gratitude, humility, and love, which flow from his knowledge that he depends upon God's grace in all things. This is what Paul means by the new freedom from the condemnation of the law. It is the freedom of a devotion to God who empowers us to live as his new people. Forgiveness, we should stress, is indeed a personal and individual experience, but it is also a community-creating experience. The church as the new people in history is created by the work of the divine mercy. The common confession of dependence upon grace is the bond of our life together in the church. It is therefore all the more sad and incomprehensible when churches claim for themselves a righteousness that belongs to God alone.

What we are talking about here is the center of Christian faith and experience. All words are inadequate. The meaning of Jesus' victory can be known only as we find in our own life the faith in that victory which does transform our spirits, our attitudes, restore our sanity, and give us a sure hope no matter what happens. Unless we find a personal participation in the meaning of the Christian story it remains for us an arbitrary assertion that may or may not be true, but that really does not matter. In Luke 6:46, Jesus puts the ultimate test of recognition of who he is in practical action: "Why do you call me 'Lord, Lord,' and not do what I tell you?" Paul describes the life of faith in these experiential terms: "always carrying in the body the death of Jesus, so that the life of Jesus may also be manifested in our bodies" (2 Cor. 4:10).

*Reconciling the world to himself.* This phrase seems a recapitulation of what has gone before, and in a sense it is. God's victory is his reconciliation of the world. But the Statement puts the meaning of the victory in the context of all time and history. What God has done in Christ is what he continues to do in the whole of his creation. We notice that the form of the verb here is "reconciling," not the simpler "reconciled." An important aspect of the Christian faith is at stake, for there is certainly a sense in which we speak of reconciliation as already accomplished. Jesus Christ is the center of history. To be in him is to be a new creation. Yet to speak of reconciliation only as what God has already accomplished would be, the authors of the Statement clearly believe, to say too little about the continuing work of God. In the first days of the church, men expected the Lord to return before any of the saints died. The fact that life went on and death continued became a source of bewilderment. The church had to work out a view of history in which the time between the life of Jesus and the end of history is the time for the preaching of the gospel to all the world. History does go on and not only the church but every individual needs the continued purging, judgment, and renewal which God gives. Sin persists, and there are new and powerful temptations for those who have been granted a taste of grace and its symbols. So Christian worship includes the continual confession of sin and prayer for grace for the world and for the church.

In the Christian faith, therefore, we are always seeking a fuller knowledge of God's work in history. There is no neat formula for understanding the progress of reconciliation. The kingdom is both present and future. Thus faith faces the future, in its immediate hopes and problems and in its ultimate mystery, believing that what God has begun in Christ will continue until the end. What such an ending may be, we can speak about only in the hopeful and triumphant symbols that point to resurrection, to final judgment, and to the time when God will be all in all.[10]

We may add one further comment. When the Statement speaks of the "world," it suggests not only our human world but the whole creation. Nature as well as man is the object of God's concern and of his creative and redemptive work. We

[10] We return to this theme on pp. 117–19.

certainly do not see very far into what this may mean. Yet as human life goes on and man's knowledge and power grow, the life of man is ever more intimately bound up with the course of nature. Nothing in the universe is beyond man's interest or exploration. From the vast interstellar spaces to the minute complexity within the atom, man seeks to find himself at home as the creative discoverer and user of his environment, who can also spoil and deface that environment if he approaches it irresponsibly. In Christianity it is the Eastern Orthodox communion that has most emphatically insisted that redemption is a cosmic process, and that we should think of the whole realm of nature as the subject of God's redemptive action. Our scientific and technologically minded century may find new direction and hope in that doctrine as we consider what it means to say that God is reconciling the world to himself.

# He Bestows
# His Spirit

*He bestows upon us his Holy Spirit,*
*creating and renewing the church of Jesus Christ,*
*binding in covenant faithful people of all ages,*
*tongues, and races.*

The experience of the Holy Spirit is one of the most powerful certainties of the faith of the New Testament. When Christians of that time reported the deeds of God, they gave a prominent place to the gift of the Spirit. Today many Christians are vague, unsure, even embarrassed by mention of the Holy Spirit. The difficulty is partly a matter of experience—and we must be honest about our experience when it differs from that of the past—and partly a matter of understanding.

Let us start, therefore, by looking at the experience of men in the community of faith. Then we can check this experience against the specific testimony of scripture.

Christians—sometimes like men of many faiths, yet in their own characteristic ways—know that they are not alone in the world. God is not an absentee landlord, who owns the place but never visits it. He is not a creator who long ago started everything going and then left it alone. He is not a remote ruler who once (in biblical times) took an active part in history, then actually entered it in a son, but then left the world.

Sometimes, of course, Christians feel the distance of God. They may say with Job (23:6), "Oh, that I knew where I might find him!" Unlike Job, they are likely to say this sentimentally, assuming that the presence of God is an entirely pleasant experience. If they get out of the sentimental mood, they may recognize the disturbing presence of God. But, whether pleasant or disturbing, the presence of God is part of the Christian experience.

God is not always vividly near—certainly not in the ways people might like. Nor can men control the experience of his presence; "the wind blows where it wills" (John 3:8).[11] But Christians believe, on the basis of their own experience and the experience of their forefathers in the faith, that God is present, recognized or unrecognized, in judgment and in mercy. One way of designating the presence of God among his people is the doctrine of the Holy Spirit.

*The biblical testimony to the Spirit.* The Bible does not offer a neat and precise account of the Holy Spirit. Instead there are two different threads of thought, sometimes interwoven and sometimes distinct.

One of these threads is very specifically associated with Pentecost. It is described in the Acts of the Apostles, chapter 2. The followers of Jesus were gathered in a room. Jesus was no longer with them—at least in anything like the sense that he had been in the days when they had known him in Galilee and

[11] The Greek word for wind in this sentence is the same as the word for spirit.

around Jerusalem. Then "suddenly," we are told, "like the rush of a mighty wind," the Holy Spirit came upon them. The experience was one of intense enthusiasm and of power. It was as though "tongues of fire" were resting on each person. They "spoke with tongues"—a phenomenon of ecstatic expression that is sometimes called *glossolalia*. Their fervor attracted a crowd, and Peter preached to those who gathered. Many of them believed his message and were baptized. Pentecost became known as the birthday of the church.

These early Christians interpreted this event as the fulfillment of a prophecy of Joel, in which God had declared, "I will pour out my Spirit upon all flesh." They also understood it as the outcome of a promise of Jesus that, when he was gone, God the Father would send "another Counselor"—the Spirit of truth, or the Holy Spirit (John 14:16, 24).

Thereafter the experience of the Holy Spirit was powerful in the life of the early church. Although some baptized persons did not immediately experience the Spirit (Acts 8:14–17; 19:1–7) and others were visited by the Spirit before baptism (Acts 10:44–48), the usual expectation was that the Spirit would come upon men at the time of baptism. Men looked to the Spirit for divine power and for guidance in making decisions. Often the external signs of the Spirit included highly emotional behavior.

Today we tend to distrust emotionalism and exaggerated religious behavior. It may be that we are so emotionally inhibited that we deprive ourselves of something authentic. On the other hand, we know that men's feelings and behavior are culturally conditioned, and we should neither expect nor reject the specific signs of God's presence that men found in the past.

We may take comfort from the fact that the apostle Paul, like most of us, distrusted excessive emotionalism. He was able to "let go" in a way that most of us cannot, and he shared the ecstatic experiences of churchmen in his time. But he was critical of the kind of fervor that took the place of love or that spread confusion instead of clarity in the church (1 Corinthians 14). And he saw the fruit of the Spirit in love, joy, and peace more convincingly than in emotional outbursts (Galatians 5:22 –24).

Thus far we have been considering the specific experience of the Holy Spirit following the life of Christ upon earth. Now we need to look at the second thread of biblical thought—a thread that shows that the activity of the Spirit is not something entirely new and unique to the time after Jesus. At the baptism of Jesus himself, we are told, the Holy Spirit descended upon him (Matt. 3:16; Luke 2:25), and soon after, Jesus went into the wilderness "full of the Holy Spirit" (Luke 4:1).

When Jesus spoke in the synagogue at Nazareth, he read from the book of the prophet Isaiah:

> "The Spirit of the Lord is upon me,
>    because he has anointed me to preach good news
>       to the poor."
>                    —Luke 4:18 (see Isaiah 61:1)

Surely this Spirit of the Lord, known to the Old Testament, and the Holy Spirit of the New Testament are not two different spirits. The Christians at Pentecost understood the two to be the same: the Holy Spirit was the same as "my Spirit" in Joel.

Recognizing this identity, we find that the Old Testament has many references to the Spirit. Several of the prophets wrote of the Spirit. (The Nicene Creed holds that the Holy Spirit "spoke through the prophets.") Job said, "The spirit of God has made me" (Job 33:4). One psalmist in Psalm 139:7, recognizing that God is everywhere, asked: "Whither shall I go from thy Spirit?" Another prayed: "Take not thy holy Spirit from me" (Ps. 51:11). Peter in the New Testament says that the Holy Spirit has spoken through David (Acts 1:16).

The two threads of thought come together in the declaration, "God is spirit" (John 4:24). The Holy Spirit is not someone other than God, not some deputy whom God sends when he cannot be bothered himself. The Holy Spirit is God, the Spirit of God, the same Spirit who is mentioned in the second verse of the Bible. Yet, just as the Christian experience of God is always related to God's activity in Christ, so the peculiarly Christian experience of the Holy Spirit derives from the knowledge of Christ. The Holy Spirit at Pentecost is no new invention, no Spirit who has never before been known. But the Holy Spirit at Pentecost comes to men—and is recognized—in a new and unprecedented way.

*The free movement of the Spirit.* In the Statement of Faith the words "Holy Spirit" are first used in the fifth declaration of God's deeds. Here the Statement follows the traditional sequence of the biblical record and of Christian declarations. God, after his act in Christ, bestows his Spirit at Pentecost, when the church begins its missionary outreach and growth.

But the God who here bestows his Spirit is the same God who has been identified in the opening confession as "the Eternal Spirit, Father of our Lord Jesus Christ and our Father." All the acts of God recorded in the Statement are acts of the God who is Holy Spirit.

The distinguished theologian Henry P. Van Dusen once criticized the Statement of Faith (before its final adoption) for tying the work of the Holy Spirit too closely to the church. He recalled that the Holy Spirit works not only in the organized church but stirs the faith of creative rebels who are more sensitive than the church and who disturb the church.[12] Such a criticism deserves to be taken seriously. It is certainly accurate in describing the activity of the Holy Spirit, who cannot be confined within any human boundaries. Christians must be alert to the movings of the Spirit outside the organizations that are called churches, even against these organizations.

[12] Henry P. Van Dusen, "The Holy Spirit and the United Church," *United Church Herald*, September 17, 1959, pp. 8–9, 31–32.

The Statement, in affirming the work of the Spirit in the church, does not throw doubt upon the work of the Spirit elsewhere. Christians are monotheists; they believe in one God who is Spirit. This God—who creates, who judges and saves, who came among us in Jesus Christ—came in a quite specific way at Pentecost. He continues to come, "creating and renewing the church of Jesus Christ." He continues to call us to responsibility and to unite men in faith.

The Bible refers to the activity of the Holy Spirit prior to the birth of Jesus—in Old Testament history. What are Christians to say of the activity of the Holy Spirit in the whole human race—among the people untouched by any influence of the Bible or any knowledge of Christianity?

The Statement of Faith does not specifically take up that issue. But it affirms that God seeks to save "all people," that he "judges men and nations." The New Testament maintains that among "all the nations" God "did not leave himself without witness" (Acts 14:16, 17). Certainly it is consistent with these beliefs to look, as Christians since the earliest times have looked, for signs of the Holy Spirit among non-Christian people. Faith in God does not entitle people to be possessive about him. Nor does belief in the free working of the Spirit diminish the importance of God's specific activity in Christ. Rather it is in Christ that Christians find the clue to discerning God's activity everywhere.

At the same time we must realize that recognition of God's work "at large" does not relieve Christians of their specific responsibility to him and to his creatures. God bestows his Holy Spirit, "creating and renewing the church of Jesus Christ."

*The Spirit and the church.* The Statement of Faith gives no formal definition of the church. It prescribes no specific form of organization, no doctrine of the ordained ministry, no location of authority. Such questions are not unimportant. But they were never part of the kerygma, the core declaration of the Christian gospel. They are under continuous discussion in the United Church of Christ, as this church seeks to understand itself and as it enters into conversation with other churches. Meanwhile the United Church makes certain definite declarations about the church. Four such declarations are plainly implied in this article of the Statement.

1. It is God who by his Holy Spirit creates the church. This church is not a creation of, and therefore is not a possession of, men.

At this point appearances may be deceptive. The church, as it is commonly recognized in its institutional expressions, is a voluntary association of people. Men may join it or leave it of their own free choice. Its policies are determined by its membership through congregational meetings and representative bodies. The members have sometimes decided, therefore, that they had the right to do with the church as they pleased. They have excluded fellow Christians from "their" church, have turned their back upon opportunities for service, have tried to make the church into a congenial club of like-minded people.

But all this is to play false with the Lord of the church. The Christian faith maintains that God has created the church. It is in response to him that men gather for worship and work in his church. He has given them freedom, by which they may defy him in the church as well as outside it. But when churches defy God, they falsify their nature and calling.

2. The same Holy Spirit ceaselessly works for the renewal of the church. The church in its human frailty errs, sins, drifts in inertia. Already in New Testament times an apostle declared, "The time has come for judgment to begin with the household of God" (1 Peter 4:17). The church is always under judgment, constantly in need of renewal. And renewal goes on continuously. An honored motto refers to the church as *ecclesia re-*

*formata, semper reformanda*—the church, reformed, always undergoing reformation.

Sometimes the renewal of the church goes on in especially notable and invigorating movements. We may think of Francis of Assisi, of the Reformation, of the confessional church affirming its faith at Barmen despite Hitler's threats, of Pope John XXIII and the Second Vatican Council, of current local and international ferments that take the church out of conventional patterns and reshape it to meet the special challenges of the contemporary world.

Churches can be guilty of all the sin and mediocrity that abound in human nature. But God's church, in a distinctive way, lives under the mandate for renewal and acknowledges the renewing power of the Holy Spirit.

3. The church is a covenant people. The meaning of the covenant has special importance in the United Church of Christ, because many of its local churches were established when Christians came together and entered into a covenant, declaring their purposes and accepting their responsibilities. Behind this practice lies the far older meaning of covenant, which is shared throughout the church.

The significance of the covenant is rooted deep in the Old Testament, which tells of God's covenant with men—with Noah, with Abraham, above all with Moses and the children of Israel. The prophets repeatedly called on the people to be true to the covenant. Jeremiah prophesied the day of the new covenant—a covenant written in the hearts of men, a covenant rising out of God's forgiveness (Jeremiah 31:31–34). And, as the apostle Paul tells us, "the Lord Jesus on the night when he was betrayed" said: "This cup is the new covenant in my blood" (1 Cor. 11:25). Actually the phrases "Old Testament" and "New Testament" might more accurately be translated "Old Covenant" and "New Covenant."

Since the word covenant is often used of legal contracts—sometimes of real estate covenants that express human prejudice

—it is important for the church to remember the nature of its covenant-belief. The Christian covenant is not simply an agreement between consenting people, who are free to break it by mutual agreement. It is a covenant between people of faith and God, the creator and renewer of the church.

4. The covenant binds "faithful people of all ages, tongues, and races."

The church, which often needs to be reminded of its contemporary responsibilities, sometimes needs to remember also that it is not merely contemporary. It includes—today— the great cloud of witnesses (Hebrews 12:1) who stretch back through the centuries. The covenant is far older than the United States of America, the British Empire—older than any nation now existing. "Faithful people of all ages" constitute the church. We today must live in our time, as men of the past lived in theirs. But we are what we are because we stand in this long succession.

One of the ancient hymns of praise, the *Te Deum*, long used in Latin and now in English, says:

The glorious company of the apostles praise thee.

The goodly fellowship of the prophets praise thee.

The noble army of martyrs praise thee.

It is this assembly of apostles, prophets, and martyrs—along with many lesser people of faith—who constitute the church.

Likewise the church includes people of all tongues and races. On Pentecost, it is reported, the Holy Spirit enabled men of different languages to understand one another. Ever since, the Holy Spirit has continued that work. Today, despite the remarkable techniques of linguistic science and simultaneous translation, languages separate people—sometimes with barriers that can be overcome only by the Holy Spirit.

Early in its history the church welcomed into its membership Jews and Greeks, Romans and Ethiopians, slaves and freemen of many nations. The book of Revelation foresaw the church as "a great multitude which no man could number, from every nation, from all tribes and peoples and tongues" (Rev. 7:9). That vision is still unfulfilled; yet it has in significant degree been realized. The church, which to its shame has sometimes heightened strife among men, has also reconciled men across national and racial hostilities. Today, in the midst of racial strife and wars hot or cold, Christians pray for those who differ with them. They recognize their unity in Christ and they strive for reconciliation.

It is a strange heresy that rejects racial equality—or that regards it as a peculiar concern of "social action" that can be neglected by some churchmen. Christians are bound by a covenant with God to their brothers in the faith, regardless of race, tongue, or nation.

The Statement of Faith warns every church that excludes men on racial grounds that such a church is violating its covenant. It reminds every church that "happens to be" of one race that something is wrong when in a multiracial society Christians are not conquering racial barriers.

The church, let us repeat, is not the possession of its members. It is created and renewed by God's Holy Spirit.

# He Calls to Discipleship

*He calls us into his church*
> *to accept the cost and joy of discipleship,*
> *to be his servants in the service of men,*
> *to proclaim the gospel to all the world*
>    *and resist the powers of evil,*
> *to share in Christ's baptism and eat at his table,*
> *to join him in his passion and victory.*

The covenant-community of the church is a missionary community. The word mission comes from a Latin verb that means *send*. To have a mission is to be sent. God creates the church by gathering and binding in a covenant those who respond to his work in Christ. God sends the church on a mission. The church is a gathered-and-sent community.

The mission of the church—this is the remarkable fact that must cause the church always to wonder—is the mission of Christ. The church, of course, is subordinate to Christ; its mission is one of discipleship. But that mission is a participation in his mission.

We have already seen Paul's description of this mission. "In Christ God was reconciling the world to himself." Furthermore Paul says that God through Christ "gave us the ministry of reconciliation" (2 Cor. 5:18). The church carries on the activity of Christ. It is, in another phrase from the New Testament, "the body of Christ" in the world today. Like any collection of human beings, it is many other things as well, and some of these interfere with its mission. Yet the very criticism that we make of the church comes from the recognition of its high calling.

*Cost and joy.* The call to discipleship reminds us of Jesus, who called the first disciples in the neighborhood of Lake Galilee. The records of the call of the first disciples are tantalizingly brief. If we look at the earliest of the Gospels, we find reports of three occasions when Jesus called disciples:

1. Seeing Simon and Andrew fishing, Jesus said, "Follow me and I will make you become fishers of men." A little later he saw James and John in a fishing boat, and "he called them." In both cases the disciples followed him "immediately." (See Mark 1:16–20.)
2. Seeing Levi at the tax office, Jesus said, "Follow me." Levi "rose and followed him" (Mark 2:14).
3. A little later we read this: "And he went up into the hills, and called to him those whom he desired; and they came to him. And he appointed twelve, to be with him, and to be sent out to preach and have authority to cast out demons" (Mark 3:13–15).

In this cryptic record one thing is clear. The disciples are a called-and-sent group. They gather around Jesus; in shared experiences they come to know and trust him. But they are not permitted to remain basking in the warm glow of friendship and the ecstasy of religious experience—although on one occasion they wanted to do just that (Mark 9:5). They are called to a mission.

The scripture does not stop to tell what persuasion Jesus used in drawing men away from their work and families to follow him. Elsewhere we see that he did not lure them with promises of prestige or affluent living. Sometimes he rebuffed the enthusiast who thought he wanted to follow Jesus but did not realize what a radical venture he was about to get into. Discipleship meant discipline, commitment, and danger. According to tradition the first twelve disciples (excepting only Judas Iscariot) became martyrs for Christ. Centuries later another Christian, Dietrich Bonhoeffer, after writing a book called *The Cost of Discipleship*, found that his faithfulness led him into concentration camp and death by hanging. Discipleship is costly.

But God calls us "to accept the cost and *joy* of discipleship." Jesus led his disciples in a life not of grim duty but of eager opportunity. He came that men might "have life, and have it abundantly" (John 10:10).

In the Beatitudes at the beginning of the Sermon on the Mount, Jesus expresses the joy of the life into which he calls men (Matthew 5:3-11). Blessed, he says, are the poor in spirit, the merciful, the pure in heart, the peacemakers. Blessed are those who hunger for righteousness and those who are persecuted for righteousness' sake. Our English translation, *blessed*, sounds a little more pious than the Greek word in the New Testament. The writers of the Gospels, reporting Jesus' sayings, used one of the two Greek words for *happy*—not the ordinary word for happiness, but the word for exuberant joy.

In a world where church membership is often a commonplace, the Statement of Faith reminds us that God "calls us into his church to accept the cost and joy of discipleship." Those who are called are also sent. A disciple (learner) is an apostle (messenger). God today calls disciples and apostles.

Some churches put great emphasis on the doctrine of "apostolic succession." By it they sometimes mean that the office of bishop continues through the ages the witness and authority of the apostles. This conception serves to remind the church of its origin and its historic continuity. But the Protestant emphasis is on another aspect of the apostolic character of the church. All Christ's followers live in an apostolic succession, called to be his disciples and apostles in a mission that is both costly and joyful. (See pages 71–72.)

*Servants in service.* In the Christian vocabulary the word servant has a quite distinctive meaning. Like much of the characteristic Christian language, this word is lifted from ordinary use. A servant is somebody who does a job for somebody else. In biblical times he might be either a slave or a hired servant—and the language of the time does not always distinguish between the two. But biblical writers, starting in the Old Testament and continuing in the New, gave the common word a special meaning.

We have already looked at the theme of the Suffering Servant expressed in several poems in the book of Isaiah.[13] We have seen that God's Suffering Servant has a healing and saving vocation for mankind. It may be that Jesus, who knew the book of Isaiah well, consciously conceived his ministry in the light of the figure of the Suffering Servant. What is sure is that Jesus' followers found these poems helpful in their understanding of him. They had hailed Jesus as Messiah (Christ). The Messiah was expected to be a heroic king, a conqueror, a

13 See Isaiah 42:1–7; 49:1–6; 50:4–9; 52:13—53:12. See pp. 69–70 above.

ruler who would establish justice. Jesus, contrary to messianic expectations, died on a cross. His followers might have decided that he was not really the Messiah they looked for. Instead they transformed their idea of Messiah into that of a Suffering Servant who is yet Lord. One of the earliest Christian liturgies, included in the letter to the Philippians, says that Christ, "taking the form of a servant . . . humbled himself and became obedient unto death, even death on a cross" (Phil. 2:7–8).

By looking at a few lines from the Songs of the Suffering Servant, we can see how powerfully the ordinary idea of the servant has been transformed and how deeply this theme has influenced Christian faith.

> Behold my servant, whom I uphold,
>   my chosen, in whom my soul delights;
> I have put my Spirit upon him,
>   he will bring forth justice to the nations.
> He will not cry or lift up his voice,
>   or make it heard in the street;
> a bruised reed he will not break,
>   and a dimly burning wick he will not quench;
>   he will faithfully bring forth justice.
> He will not fail or be discouraged
>   till he has established justice in the earth;
>   and the coastlands wait for his law.
>                                  —Isaiah 42:1–4

The Statement of Faith declares that we, following Christ, are called to be God's servants in the service of men. The mission of the church is not to seek honor and authority for itself; it is to enter into the suffering of human life, to work for justice among the nations, to bring healing and forgiveness to a sinful mankind.

*Service* has become a common word in the life of the twentieth century. Men of affairs belong to service clubs; we buy gasoline at service stations; we read advertisements that promise superior service. We should not disdain this ordinary, even commercialized use of the word. It reminds us that in the ordinary affairs of men we depend upon one another and we need service. The routines of making a living, as Jesus sometimes showed, may be parables of the Christian life.

But the parable should lead us to the deeper reality. Christ was a servant who loved, shared, and suffered. God calls his church to follow Christ. He asks us to be his servants in the service of men.

*Proclaiming the gospel.* An integral part of the reconciling ministry is the telling of the good news of Christ to the world. By placing the proclamation of the gospel in the midst of the description of the Christian mission, the Statement of Faith suggests its significance. It is not the whole mission of the church, yet it is essential to that mission.

There are times when to be God's servants in the service of men means that works of justice and love are more important than any words about faith. There are other times when the telling of the gospel is more important than any activity. No doubt there are Christians who in the diversity of gifts are especially well equipped for one task or the other. But the Christian mission is incomplete without both.

To judge from some popular talk, the aim of Christian missionary activity is simply to spread the message of Christ, and the effectiveness of missions is measured by the number of converts. But the New Testament and the teaching of Jesus do not support this judgment. On the other hand, the church is not solely a social service agency, aiming to help people but indifferent to their beliefs. Rather the church has heard the instruction, "Go therefore and make disciples of all nations" (Matt. 28:19).

Through the centuries the church has spread the news of Christ with remarkable results. A vast part of mankind has heard the message. Many have believed and have become part

of the church. The entire church in Europe and America—
the areas of Christianity's greatest numerical strength—is the
result of missionary activity. Every Christian in these areas who
values his life in the covenant-community owes gratitude to
missionaries.

The missionary story at its best has been a stirring epic.
Christians—including men of genius and very ordinary people
—have felt stirred by God to spread the news of Christ. With
no incentive of profit and no expectation of personal gain they
have accepted hardship, danger, and death. In their reconciling
ministry they have taken educational activities, agricultural
skills, and the arts of medicine with the gospel.

There have been many other factors in the spread of
Christianity, some of them quite alien to the spirit of Christ.
Kings have marched armies through rivers in mass baptisms.
Political, commercial, and military forces have hopelessly confused Christianity with imperial aims. Some men and societies
have accepted Christianity as the religion of a more advanced
or more powerful culture—a familiar phenomenon in the history of many religions.

Today that situation is passing. Increasingly the world
resents imperialism. Many societies are discovering that they
can import Western technology and weapons without im-
porting Western religion.

The church can, for the most part, be grateful for this
change. Christians will not agree with the naïve faith that
technology and weapons will solve all human problems. But
they can welcome a situation in which men can make their own
response to the Christian message, freed from economic, political, or cultural pressures.

Christians will continue to proclaim the gospel. There is
no reason at all—certainly no biblical reason—to expect all
men to accept it. In addition to the natural human resistance to
God—a resistance that Christians know in themselves as well as

outside themselves—there are two main reasons why men do not find the Christian message convincing.

The first is that Christians are often such poor representatives of the gospel. A message about reconciliation, unconnected with deeds of reconciliation, is not convincing. Christians have to their shame made Christ a symbol to many people of racial superiority, of outside domination, even of persecution. Often when people reject Christ, they are really rejecting his spokesmen. Before criticizing those who refuse allegiance to Christ, Christians need always to ask, "Is it our fault?"

The second reason is that many men in all parts of the world find significant meaning in other faiths. These may be ancient faiths, embodying the wisdom and religious insight of centuries of experience; or they may be modern faiths like agnostic humanism. The Christian mission in such cases is not to argue for the superiority of "our" religion as against "theirs." If the influence of Christ makes a Hindu more critical of caste in his own religion without converting him to Christianity, that too is a work of the ministry of reconciliation.

Even so, Christians will continue to tell the world of Christ. The aim will not be to pressure the world or to argue it into agreement. But the church cannot be silent about its Lord. In gratitude to God for his deed in Christ, Christians will tell the news of that deed and carry on the reconciling ministry. Others, hearing and seeing, may make their own responses.

The Statement of Faith at this point joins closely two phrases: "to proclaim the gospel to all the world and resist the powers of evil." This combination, which has seemed strange to some, comes directly from the work of Christ. He sent out the twelve "to preach" and "to cast out demons." The telling of the gospel inevitably means conflict with the demonic forces of our experience.

The Statement carefully avoids any suggestion that the

world is evil. It particularly rejects any theme of struggle between the church (good) and the world (bad). It has earlier affirmed that this world is God's creation. But it has recognized the reality of sin.

The proclamation of the gospel meets many responses. Sometimes the response is approval; sometimes, indifference. And sometimes it is opposition.

In this twentieth century the opposition has often been spectacular. Two examples are especially obvious: under the Nazi regime and in some situations of racial strife (particularly in the United States and in South Africa) the declaration of the gospel has been costly and dangerous for faithful Christians. The church has learned that the age of the martyrs is not restricted to ancient history. In many less conspicuous cases, too, the Christian mission encounters opposition from those who feel threatened by its call for justice and love. In the language of traditional doctrine, this is the age of the church militant, not the church triumphant.

Perhaps the most common response of "the powers of evil" is not to oppose the Christian message but to corrupt it. Men claim the gospel for their own unholy purposes, they change it into an ideology supporting their partisan interests, they build religious institutions that shield them from God. The Christian who tells the good news of Christ must resist the powers of evil that operate at large and that tempt him from within himself.

*Baptism and Lord's Supper.* The sacraments of baptism and the Lord's Supper, going back to Jesus himself, have always been major celebrations of faith and marks of the church. Curiously the classical creeds have given them little attention. The Apostles' Creed does not mention either. The Nicene Creed refers to "one baptism for the remission of sins," but says nothing about the Holy Communion.

The Statement of Faith gives attention to both of these sacraments. It does not develop a specific doctrine of the sacraments; that is an issue which the church continues to discuss. But it does put the sacraments in a context—a context that is strange to many churchmen.

In the practice of recent centuries the church has often assigned the sacraments to the inner (almost the introspective) life of the church, as contrasted with the outward reach of the Christian mission. Sometimes the church has found within itself cults of sacramentalists, who like ceremonial worship, and activists, who want to get on with the world's work. The Statement of Faith includes the sacraments within the article on God's call to mission. It relates them closely to life in the world. In this respect it seeks to be true to the meaning of the sacraments in the New Testament.

The sacraments are the acts—or some of the acts—in which Christians join themselves to Christ "in his passion and victory." The Statement has made this emphasis so strong that its wording has prompted considerable discussion and some controversy.

Is it pretentious, or even irreverent, to say that we share in Christ's baptism? Is Christ's baptism something quite different from ours?

Let us notice immediately that the Statement does not say that every ceremony of baptism is a sharing in Christ's baptism. It says instead that God "calls us . . . to share in Christ's baptism." From this point we can go on to investigate three themes in the discussion of baptism in the New Testament.

The first theme is the baptism of Jesus himself by John the Baptist, an event recorded in Matthew 3:13–17, Mark 1:9–11, and Luke 3:21–22. This baptism bothered some of the early Christians. Baptism, they thought, was for ordinary mortals; Jesus had no need of baptism. Mark and Luke never raise this issue, but Matthew does. He reports that John the Baptist protested that Jesus should not be baptized by John, but Jesus insisted on the act in order "to fulfill all righteousness." Here it seems clear that Jesus, as a genuine human being, shared with other human beings in the baptism.

The second theme arises when James and John make the foolish request for an honored place in glory. Jesus asks them whether they can be baptized with his baptism. They reply, again too brashly, that they can. Jesus answers: "With the baptism with which I am baptized, you will be baptized; but to sit at my right hand or at my left is not mine to grant" (Mark 10:39–40). Most interpreters take this to mean that Jesus is talking about a baptism of suffering that is yet to come and is saying that these disciples, despite all their present naïveté, will share in that suffering.

The third theme is developed by Paul, who understands baptism as the symbol of our death and resurrection with Christ. "We were buried therefore with him by baptism into death, so that as Christ was raised from the dead by the glory of the Father, we too might walk in newness of life" (Rom. 6:4; see Gal. 2:20).

In each of these cases the belief is that Jesus shares in human baptism or that we share in his baptism. If this discussion seems overly technical, it is all aimed at one major point. Baptism, as a sacramental and ceremonial act, is the symbol of something that is not ceremonial—the entrance into the missionary community that continues Christ's reconciling ministry and shares in his death and resurrection. Far from being an exclusively "religious" act, baptism sends the Christian into the life of the world.

Much the same may be said of the Lord's Supper. The first Lord's Supper was the meal of Jesus with his disciples the night before his crucifixion. Throughout the centuries of history new generations of disciples have repeated that act. It is known also as the Holy Communion, the Eucharist (thanksgiving), and the mass (related to mission). These names have valid and important meanings, but they have sometimes helped people to forget that the Lord's Supper is a meal. Our forms of celebrating it also tend to hide any resemblance to a common supper. But it is important to realize that the central sacrament of Christian faith is a meal—as "worldly" an act as anything that men do.

Occasionally someone has expressed surprise that the Statement of Faith uses so ordinary a word as "eat" in referring to the Lord's Supper. "Commune," for example, has been suggested as an improvement. But Jesus, according to our records, used the common word. "Take, eat," he said (Matt. 26:26). So the act of eating becomes one sign of the Christian's recognition of the cost and joy of discipleship.

Believing in God, we have said earlier, is an act of faith. Now we should add that observance of the sacraments is an act of faith. It is heartening to see the increasing agreement among Protestants and Catholics on this issue. Hans Küng, eminent Roman Catholic theologian, has written: "Neither the word nor the sacrament work automatically; if they find no faith they cannot function."[14] In infant baptism the emphasis is on the faith of the church, which thus expresses God's love for the child. In adult baptism and the Holy Communion, the emphasis is on the faith both of the individual and of the church in their response to Christ.

Baptism and the Lord's Supper are thus celebrations of Christ's passion and victory, in which the Christian is called to join. If in this chapter we have emphasized the passion, in the next we shall emphasize the victory.

[14] In John Courtney Murray (ed.), *Freedom and Man* (New York: P. J. Kenedy, 1965), p. 24.

# He
# Promises

*He promises to all who trust him*
*forgiveness of sins and fullness of grace,*
*courage in the struggle for justice and peace,*
*his presence in trial and rejoicing,*
*and eternal life in his kingdom which has no end.*

The notion of a God who makes promises is not a natural one for modern man to wrap his mind around. Yet the Bible—Old Testament and New—is full of statements about the promises of God. We read that God made promises to Abraham, that God's promises prove true, that God never lies. This anthropomorphic language seems to come out of a world vastly different from ours.

But before we jump to any conclusion, we shall be wise to investigate what God's promises meant to the men of the Bible. Granted they did not have our scientific picture of the world, they certainly reflected upon their experience as intensely as we do on ours. No doubt, when they talked of God's promises, they were less inhibited in their imagination than we. Probably they took their visions and dreams more seriously than we.

Even so, they knew that imagination, visions, and dreams are often deceptive. The prophets criticized vain imagination and wishful thinking about God. Wherever biblical man got his ideas of God, he still had to check them out with his daily experience. He had to sift the many foolish religious ideas from the few that held good.

So when he expressed his trust in the promises of God, he was not simply taking the word of some seer. He knew that the seers were wrong more often than they were right. The trust in God's promises must have been based on the confirmation of experience. Some claims for God's promises were quickly smashed. Some held up for many generations, then collapsed. A few stood the test of long experience in good times and bad.

We might make a comparison with a modern astronaut, who trusts that his spaceship will stay in orbit and will not capriciously hurtle out into interplanetary space. We can quickly see the difference between the astronaut's trust in the processes of nature and biblical man's trust in God. The former can be tested by measurements and experiments that are publicly verifiable; the latter, even though it is the experience of a community and not merely of an individual, is not testable by the same devices. But in both cases there is an assurance that is validated in experience.

The biblical faith in God's promises does not depend, in the last analysis, on the reports of anybody about what God secretly told him. It depends upon the conviction of a community of faith about the character of God. To say that God keeps his promises is to say that he is faithful and reliable, that his character as revealed to men is constant, that he can be trusted. That is why Paul can write to his friends at Corinth that "God is faithful" (2 Cor. 1:18) and that "all the promises of God find their Yes" in Christ (2 Cor. 1:20). That is why contemporary Christians, no less than biblical men, can talk of the promises of God. Of course, we do not simply take the word of men of the past. We have the same responsibility they had to sift out truth from imagination.

The Statement of Faith affirms four promises of God to "all who trust him."

*Forgiveness and grace.* Here the Statement builds upon its earlier affirmations. God, who "seeks in holy love to save all people from aimlessness and sin," has "come to us" in Jesus Christ, "conquering sin and death and reconciling the world to himself." That is why Christians can go on to say that God promises "forgiveness and grace" to those who trust him.

Let us look first at the experience of grace. Like a few other words in the Christian vocabulary, grace has a meaning and tone that cannot be translated into any other language. But, again like others of the words of faith, this one has roots in an ordinary, everyday meaning. We see it in the trio of words: grace, gracious, and graceful. A gracious act is done generously, magnanimously, with goodwill. A graceful act is beautiful, poised, and free. If a man merely lives up to the letter of a contract or if he grudgingly does a good deed, his act is neither gracious nor graceful. An act of grace goes beyond any requirements; it is done freely and in good spirit for the sake of another.

God's grace is his outgoing love—love beyond man's deserving, love freely given, love that is concerned for the good of man rather than the prerogatives of God. It is not sentimental love that protects man from hardships; it is constant love in the midst of prosperity or hardship. The Christian affirmation is that God extends such love to man, that he confers such love upon man so that man can himself act graciously.

In the Christian tradition grace is understood in two ways: as forgiveness and as illumination and power. Here we are thinking about grace as the forgiveness of sins. A little later we shall think about it as power.

In the Lord's Prayer, as recorded by Luke, Jesus directs us to say: "Forgive us our sins, for we ourselves forgive every one who is indebted to us" (Luke 11:4). It might be better if we used that language rather than the more abstract language of debts. But Luke's version requires us to make a claim that most of us would find difficult: "We ourselves forgive every one who is indebted to us." Matthew is not much gentler: "Forgive us our debts, as we also have forgiven our debtors" (Matt. 6:12).

Most of us, if we pray honestly, ask for something more than that. We should like God to forgive us before checking to be sure that we have forgiven all who have offended us. Indeed, part of the very sin that we need to be forgiven is our inability to forgive others.

God, as we know him in Christ, does that. As Jesus said, "I came not to call the righteous, but sinners" (Matt. 9:13). Forgiveness extends to the prodigal son, to the guilty tax collector whose only prayer was "God be merciful to me a sinner," to the repentant thief on the cross.

In modern sophisticated society we often seek to get rid of "guilt complexes"—a good idea, no doubt. But often it is easier to get rid of the complex than of the guilt. The good news is that God offers forgiveness. "If we say we have no sin, we deceive ourselves, and the truth is not in us. If we confess our sins, he is faithful and just, and will forgive our sins and cleanse us from all unrighteousness" (1 John 1:8–10). That forgiveness does not relieve us of all responsibility. Our sins are costly—to those we have harmed, to ourselves, and to God. But in the assurance of forgiveness, we find ourselves more ready to forgive others. In the healing of forgiveness, we are better able to live as whole men. The grace of forgiveness becomes the grace of power.

*Courage in struggle.* Another of God's promises is "courage in the struggle for justice and peace." There are two kinds of peace in Christian thinking; and although they are related, they must not be confused. The first is a peace, an inner serenity, that comes from trust in God. It is a peace that endures in the midst of outer conflict and peril. It is "the peace of God, which passes all understanding" (Phil. 4:7), "the peace of Christ" that may rule in men's hearts (Col. 3:15). This peace is not attained through struggle. It is a gift of grace—although like all gifts of grace it requires a response from us.

The second kind of peace is political—peace among the nations and among the people within the nations. It is a peace based on justice. It is the peace of the prophecy:

> They shall beat their swords into plowshares,
> and their spears into pruning hooks;
> nation shall not lift up sword against nation,
> neither shall they learn war any more.
> —Isaiah 2:4

This peace is also a gift. As Isaiah describes it, it is an eschatological peace; that is, an ultimate hope that is never entirely realized in human history but that can influence our conduct now.

At this point, human efforts can make a big difference. There are policies that make for injustice and war, and policies that make for justice and peace. A great and prosperous nation can save people in other lands from starvation, can help to raise standards of living, can improve educational opportunities, can offer to settle disputes through international organizations rather than through threats and warfare, can strive for justice throughout the world. None of these policies can guarantee peace. But they can make a difference. It is not enough that Christians pray for peace. They must work. They must enter into "the struggle for justice and peace." And their prayers will be not for some divine intervention that will suddenly end war; the prayers will be for courage and wisdom in the struggle.

We have been considering justice and peace together, because they belong together. Sometimes, of course, men seek a shortcut that achieves peace without justice. But, as Augustine wrote in *The City of God*, an unjust peace is not truly peace. It is a spurious imitation of peace. And it will not endure. The reason is that God "judges men and nations by his righteous will."

Hence we return to the prophetic demand that we have emphasized earlier. The Hebrew prophets knew that no evasions and no pious ceremonies could satisfy God's requirement of justice.

"Take away from me the noise of your songs;
to the melody of your harps I will not listen.
But let justice roll down like waters,
and righteousness like an everflowing stream."
—Amos 5:23–24

He has showed you, O man, what is good;
and what does the Lord require of you
but to do justice, and to love kindness,
and to walk humbly with your God?
—Micah 6:8

Jesus continued this prophetic heritage. He criticized the churchmen of his time because they performed their religious duties with meticulous care but "neglected the weightier matters of the law, justice and mercy and faith" (Matt. 23:23). He brought "good news to the poor" and to "those who are oppressed" (Luke 4:18).

If his church is faithful to him, it will take up the cause of those who suffer from poverty, racial discrimination, and oppression. Sometimes the church does that. Too often it forgets. Over the course of time the church has become one of the established institutions of society. It is made up largely of the people who have a fairly good position in the society and are therefore content with things as they are. They tend to resent any change—even a change for justice—that disturbs the social order or threatens their privileges.

Karl Marx maintained that men's ideas of right and wrong, and their whole outlook upon the world, are determined largely by their economic interests. It is easier to argue with Marx than to demonstrate by actions that he is wrong. Christians refute

Marx whenever they think and act for the sake of justice, even though that justice will help others more than themselves.

It is easy for even well-meaning Christians to deceive themselves on issues like this. For example, the white Christian may favor racial justice even at the cost of losing his privileged position in society. But in a time of social change, which is almost always a time of confusion and strife, he is likely to value peace—even unjust peace—above justice. The prosperous Christian may theoretically favor justice for the poor, but he can easily find objections to specific antipoverty programs. The American society with its wealth and power may still believe in "liberty and justice for all"; but we may have trouble understanding the aspirations of people who are more eager for justice than for a smooth-running world.

At such times peace, detached from justice, easily becomes the ideology of the comfortable. Christians have special reason to be on their guard against this temptation. Long ago Jeremiah warned the people of his time:

> "They have healed the wound of my people lightly,
>     saying, 'Peace, peace,'
>   when there is no peace."
>
> —Jeremiah 6:14

The Prince of Peace actually brought disruption into the world. On one occasion he said: "Do not think that I have come to bring peace on earth; I have not come to bring peace, but a sword" (Matt. 10:34).

That last statement, of course, has been taken out of context to justify all kinds of hostility, including coercion with no aim of reconciliation. The point is that justice and peace alike belong in a context that includes both. The ministry of reconciliation, as the life of Jesus shows, sometimes brings disturbance and strife that upset the smooth running of society. Yet its purpose remains, in the most profound sense, peace.

So Christians are called to act for justice and peace. God does not promise them success. Evil is persistent in our world, and success is never sure. God's promise is courage in the struggle.

*His presence.* The promise includes "his presence in trial and rejoicing." Life knows both. In a precarious existence we never know which tomorrow will bring.

It is strange that Christians have sometimes expected that their faith and obedience would spare them from trials. They should know that human beings are creatures, that life is uncertain, sometimes painful, and always mortal. In pain and death we learn what it is to be men and not gods.

We may reason that the Christian life is likely to avoid some of the sufferings that can be called "the wages of sin." Some of the Christian virtues are prudential virtues, helpful in the business of living. But the Christian life also involves men in responsibilities and risks that a shrewd self-interest can easily avoid. As Jesus walked knowingly into life's trials, his followers will do the same.

The influence of Christianity upon the world has brought relief to some sufferings. Works of mercy and the spread of a humanitarian spirit have lifted burdens from mankind. Yet the twentieth century has brought intense suffering to millions of people, usually without regard to their faith, sometimes specifically because of their faith.

Christians in countries of relative freedom and security know that they are bound in the covenant community to Christians who have maintained their faith through persecution. The fortunate need to remember their brothers in peril, but they need to remember also the trials of prosperity. At one meeting between American churchmen and Christians from "behind the iron curtain," an American said something about praying for the East Europeans. The reply came gently but pointedly:

"We want your prayers, if you want ours." Suddenly the Americans realized with new force the trials of life in an affluent society where the church may be smothered by kindness rather than battered by persecution.

If life has its trials, both of hardship and prosperity, it has also its occasions of authentic rejoicing. It is a mistake to so emphasize God's support in suffering as to forget him in the exultancy of life. *Joy* and *rejoicing* are among the most frequent words of scripture. Believers naturally call upon God at weddings as truly as at funerals—and not only because of the solemnity of the marriage vows but also because of the sheer joy of marital love.

Dietrich Bonhoeffer has told our generation forcefully that God consecrates our joys as genuinely as he solaces our sorrows. Writing from prison, where he had plain reason to realize the pain of life, he said that God speaks to man in his strength as well as in his weakness. Too often, he said, the church has preferred to see man remain weak in order that he would realize his dependence upon God. This is a cheap tactic. God has given us our powers; he welcomes our increasing power and freedom.[15]

Christians in a rich and powerful land are rightly troubled by their responsibilities in a needy world. But they should not feel guilty about their achievements, except as these have been won unjustly or with indifference to the needs of others. They have a right to rejoice in their attainments, to thank God for the opportunities of life, and to enjoy his presence in their rejoicing.

When we ask God's presence, whether in trial or rejoicing, he will be there. As a matter of fact, he will be there even if we do not invite him. Often it is easy to forget God; often it is convenient to ignore him. But wanted or not, God is with us in trial and rejoicing.

[15] *Letters and Papers from Prison* (New York: Macmillan, 1962), pp. 194–200, 206–10, 211–15.

*Eternal life in his kingdom.* The God of creation is the God of our final destiny. He who gave us life will not desert us at the end. This has been the affirmation of Christians ever since the first of them told the world that Christ had risen from the dead.

The way in which Christians have visualized and conceptualized their final destiny has varied. In the absence of concrete evidence, imagination has sometimes run wild. Some persons picturing life after death, both in their delight over the pleasures of the saved and in their gloating over the punishment of the wicked, have quite forgotten the nature of God's love and the meaning of trust in him.

Today our ideas of the future are likely to be more restrained than in past centuries. Theologians, studying the Statement of Faith, have observed that it included some equivalent for all the major affirmations of the Apostles' Creed, except one: "He ascended into heaven, and sitteth on the right hand of God the Father Almighty; from thence he shall come to judge the quick and the dead."

It is important that we be honest at this point—as in all our beliefs. Rather than pretend to complete agreement with traditional belief, we must say candidly that our beliefs have changed.

Just how much they have changed is hard to say. We are not certain exactly what Christians of the past meant by that sentence in the Apostles' Creed. Some believers, we assume, took the statement quite literally. Some, we know, did not.

A literal understanding of the statement, for example, would mean that God had a body with two arms, a right and a left. But the New Testament has clearly declared that God is Spirit. One of the great Christian thinkers of the past, Augustine, for a time thought that he could not accept Christian faith because he could not believe that God had a body. When he learned that orthodox faith did not require him to hold such a belief, a block to his conversion was removed.

Similarly for some Christians of the past the literal, pictorial description of Christ's return in judgment (the so-called Second Coming) was a symbolic way of saying that God is the final judge of our lives and that our ultimate destiny is with him. But probably most Christians in most centuries took the creed in a more literal fashion.

Today we are likely to be skeptical of the old attempts to describe the outcome of life and history. In part we have acquired tested knowledge that refutes some of the traditional pictures of the world; for example, as we have mentioned earlier, the three-story universe with heaven above, hell below, and the earth between. In part we have to say simply that the temper of man's thinking has changed and we are no longer convinced by some old assertions. We may be mistaken; there is no reason to think that our generation is the arbiter of truth for all time. But we have to be truthful with ourselves. It is no service of God to say things that we do not believe.

At this point it is helpful to realize that the Bible is far more restrained in its affirmations than many later believers have been. Jesus refused to elaborate on the future. His major statement about the future judgment is cast in the form of a parable; it is to be taken quite seriously, but the language of the throne and the sheep and goats is a reminder not to take the parable too literally. On another occasion, when questioned about the future, Jesus admitted candidly the limitations of his knowledge and said that only the Father knew (Matthew 24:36). More important than conjectures is the trust with which Jesus met his death. In both his acceptance of limitations and his assurance he can be our guide.

The Christian confidence is that God is eternal, that our responsibility is to him, that our destiny is in his care. His steadfast love is not defeated by our sin or our death. In Jesus Christ he has won a victory over both sin and death. Those who trust him have already begun to experience eternal life: for "this is eternal life, that they know thee the only true God, and Jesus Christ whom thou hast sent" (John 17:3).

Day in and day out, year in and year out, the church prays in the prayer of Jesus Christ: "Thy kingdom come." The prayer reminds us of the psalm that declares: "Thy kingdom is an everlasting kingdom" (Ps. 145:13). In Christ we are assured that we have a place in that kingdom. What more do we need to know?

Some churchmen want to say more than the Statement says about eternal life. That is quite appropriate. Presumably most Christians want to say more than this brief statement says on other subjects as well. It is good that they should say more— but with one warning: no elaboration of belief, whether in terms of traditional doctrine or contemporary conjecture, may take the place of the trust in God that is the basis of Christian hope. Sometimes the frantic effort to peer into the future is an evasion of the real issue: the trust in God that sustains life now and gives us confidence for our future.

With this trust we can say with the apostle Paul: "I am sure that neither death, nor life, nor angels, nor principalities, nor things present, nor things to come, nor powers, nor height, nor depth, nor anything else in all creation, will be able to separate us from the love of God in Christ Jesus our Lord" (Rom. 8:38).

Then we may want to go on, in the language of an imaginative writer who never intended to be taken so literally as some people have done, to look for the day when voices in heaven will say: "The kingdom of the world has become the kingdom of our Lord and of his Christ, and he shall reign for ever and ever" (Rev. 11:15).

# Appendixes

## The Use of the Statement

&raquo; IN THE FREE CHURCH POLITY of the United Church of Christ only one generalization can be made about the use of the Statement of Faith: It is used when Christians want to use it.

We have seen that the Statement was approved by the General Synod of the United Church in 1959 "as a testimony ... to the faith commonly held among us."[1] The General Synod submitted the Statement to conferences, associations, and churches "for their approval and use." Subsequent approval was more often by informal acceptance and use than by recorded votes.

[1] See pp. 16–17, 28.

121

The United Church of Christ is not in any technical sense a creedal church, and the use of the Statement is in no way prescribed. It is, in fact, used frequently in worship services of the General Synod and various other assemblies of the church. Many local churches use it, either regularly or on occasion (sometimes during Lent or on communion Sundays). Other churches prefer to use classical creeds; still others use no confessional statements in worship. The United Church of Christ, encouraging freedom of practice, would not have it otherwise.

The Statement is sometimes used in interdenominational college worship. Occasionally it is used by churches of other denominations. In German and Spanish versions it has been used in worship in Europe and in South America.

Many churches incorporate the Statement into study programs. Adult and youth groups in local churches or summer camps have studied it. Ministers have used it in preaching, sometimes developing a series of sermons around its main affirmations. One adult course in the United Church Curriculum, *Classical Creeds and Living Faith*, studied the Statement along with the classical creeds. A youth course, *Journey into Faith*, included study of this Statement and encouraged young people to write their own statements of faith. Some confirmation classes have built their study course around the Statement.

The Statement has been set to music and sung by choirs. It has been adapted as a hymn. It has been made into choral readings, incorporated in written dialogues, rewritten in the form of a prayer.

Such varied uses are consistent with the purpose of the Statement: to be a testimony of faith in words of our time. It is one way of confessing Christian faith, a way that some Christians find helpful. No one assumes that it was written for the ages. In time to come Christians will again and again seek to state their faith in words of their time as God gives them light.

# The Development of the Statement

This brief account of the preparation and adoption of the Statement of Faith is offered for two reasons. First, it is an important historical episode in the establishing of the United Church of Christ. Second, it is an interesting example of the way in which a denomination enters into theological discussion and seeks to discover its common mind.

In the long negotiations leading up to the union that formed the United Church of Christ, the uniting bodies had agreed that the new church would draw up a Statement of Faith. The basic purpose of that Statement, as set forth in the Basis of Union, has been described on page 16.

The Uniting General Synod, meeting in Cleveland in July, 1957, elected a commission of thirty men and women to prepare the Statement. The commission, drawn equally from the Congregational Christian Churches and the Evangelical and Reformed Church, included biblical scholars, theologians, pastors, and laymen.[2]

[2] Congregational Christian members of the commission were:

| | |
|---|---|
| John C. Bennett | Walter M. Horton |
| Ralph Hyslop | Mary Ely Lyman |
| Mrs. W. Bayard Buckham | Edward F. Manthei |
| Loring D. Chase (co-secretary) | Richard R. Niebuhr |
| Nels F. S. Ferré | Oliver Powell |
| L. K. Hall | Helen Huntington Smith |
| Roger Hazelton | Daniel D. Williams |
| Douglas Horton | |

Evangelical and Reformed members were:

| | |
|---|---|
| Elmer J. F. Arndt (chairman) | Frederick L. Herzog |
| Edward W. Brueseke | Allen O. Miller |
| Bernice A. Buehler | Robert V. Moss, Jr. (co-secretary) |
| Alfred L. Creager | John L. Schmidt |
| John P. Dillenberger | Roger L. Shinn |
| Louis H. Gunnemann | Morris D. Slifer |
| Robert G. Herrmann | Bela Vassady |
| | Beatrice M. Weaver |

The commission worked for a period of two years under the instructions in the Basis of Union, as described in Part I of this book. It began its deliberations with study of the historic confessions of the uniting churches. With these it studied several contemporary declarations of faith from churches around the world. In the course of the discussion the commission sought to gain a clearer view of the form and content that the United Church statement might take.

As a next step each member of the commission was invited to write a statement of faith. The twenty-three statements, unidentified as to authorship, were circulated among the commission. Some members tested some of the statements in local churches or conferred with other churchmen about them.

At the next meeting of the commission the officers presented a composite statement drawn from the documents that had been circulated. The commission worked over this statement in detail. It was obvious that the group would not produce a statement with appropriate unity and style by this method; but a thorough airing of issues resulted. After this discussion and study, four members of the commission were asked again to write statements, this time seeking to express the mind of the commission. The officers, working primarily on the basis of one of these statements, again presented a draft to the commission. In detailed discussion the commission went over the draft, line by line, often word by word. After thorough consideration, further work by a drafting committee, then still further revision by the commission, the Statement was presented to the United Church.[3]

The Statement was printed in the *United Church Herald, The Christian Century, The New York Times,* and other news media several months before the next General Synod. One

---

[3] A more detailed and colorful account of the commission's work up to this point, written by the Rev. Loring D. Chase, one of the co-secretaries, was published in the *United Church Herald* of March 26, 1959, and reprinted in *Classic Christian Creeds* by Paul F. Mehl (Philadelphia: United Church Press, 1964).

result was wide discussion of the Statement within the United Church and among scholars and leaders of other churches. The commission collected suggestions and criticisms from many sources.

The commission formally presented the Statement to the General Synod at Oberlin on July 6, 1959. The commission itself realized that its work was incomplete in the sense that theology is always incomplete, but it doubted that it would do better by taking more time. At the same time it was prepared to do further work if the General Synod so desired.

The mood of the General Synod obviously favored action on the report. The Synod had met with the hope of adopting a constitution for the United Church. When it became evident that the intricate work of the constitution could not be completed but would have to be delayed until an adjourned session a year later, the Synod became especially eager to adopt a Statement of Faith. Some delegates welcomed the schedule as a sign that agreement on faith should precede agreement on the constitution.[4]

Friendly discussion, debate, and questioning on the Statement came from the floor of the Synod. On one evening, following a session of the Synod, the commission held an open hearing extending late into the night, to give opportunity for more detailed discussion by delegates to the Synod. There was no doubt that delegates wanted to discuss the Statement and that the commission took their comments seriously.

The commission continued its meetings during the Synod, considering both the judgments of the delegates and the many other comments that had been received. One session was given to consideration of criticisms that had come from the Evangelical Church of the Union in Germany, where a committee had translated the Statement into New Testament Greek and studied it.

[4] See Harold E. Fey's news report in *The Christian Century*, July 22, 1959.

In these final meetings, as in all the preceding ones, the discussion was spirited. Clashes of opinion were common. But the discussions never produced factions committed to fixed positions. Specifically there was never an issue on which denominational divisions occurred; every question that divided the group also divided the two denominational contingents. Where opinions differed, the usual procedure was to work toward a consensus. On a few occasions a matter was settled by a vote, and probably everyone on the commission found himself in the minority at some time. More remarkable was the common mind that emerged and expressed itself in the final unanimous vote recommending the Statement to the General Synod.

On July 8 the commission brought back to the General Synod a Statement revised at three points from its earlier report. Further discussion from the floor followed. Then the Synod voted approval of the Statement. The specific terms of the motion have been indicated on page 17. The minutes of the General Synod report: "The delegates responded to the agreement on the Statement of Faith by standing and joining voices in the singing of the Doxology. Chairman Arndt was called upon to lead in a unison reading of the Statement."

## The Statement in Translation

The Statement of Faith has been used liturgically in German and Spanish versions. For reasons of theological interest it has been translated into New Testament Greek. Thanks are due the many persons who have been consulted in the translations below, but in each case the translator listed took the major responsibility.

## Glaubensbezeugung

Wir glauben an Gott, den ewigen Geist, den Vater unseres
Herrn Jesus Christus und unseren Vater, und wir bezeugen
seine Taten:

Er ruft die Welten ins Dasein,
  schafft den Menschen nach seinem eigenen Bild
  und zeigt ihm den Weg des Lebens und den Weg des
  Todes.

Er sucht in heiliger Liebe alle Menschen zu retten von Ziello-
  sigkeit und Sünde.
Er richtet Menschen und Völker nach seinem gerechten
  Willen verkündet durch Propheten und Apostel.

In Jesus Christus, dem Mann von Nazareth, unserem gekreu-
  zigten und auferstandenen Herrn,
  kam er zu uns
  und nahm teil an unserem Los,
  überwindet Sünde und Tod
  und versöhnt die Welt mit sich selbst.

Er verleiht uns seinen Heiligen Geist,
  schafft und erneuert die Kirche Jesu Christi,
  vereint in seinem Bund glaubende Menschen aller Zeiten,
  Sprachen, und Rassen.

Er ruft uns in seine Kirche,
  damit wir Opfer und Freude der Nachfolge bejahen,
  damit wir seine Diener sind im Dienst an Menschen,

damit wir das Evangelium aller Welt verkünden
und den Mächten des Bösen widerstehen,
damit wir teilhaben an Christi Taufe und an seinem Tische
essen,
damit wir mit ihm verbunden sind in seinem Leiden und
in seinem Sieg.

Er verspricht allen, die ihm vertrauen,
Vergebung der Sünden und Gnade die Fülle,
Mut im Kampf für Gerechtigkeit und Frieden,
seine Gegenwart in Anfechtung und Freude
und ewiges Leben in seinem Reich, das kein Ende hat.

Ihm sei Lob und Ehre, Ruhm und Macht. Amen.

Translated by Hanns Peter Keiling
University of Göttingen, West Germany

## Afirmacion de Fe

Creemos en Dios, el Espíritu Eterno, Padre de nuestro Señor
Jesucristo y Padre nuestro, de cuyas obras testificamos:

El por su palabra crea los mundos,
  crea al hombre a su propia imagen
  y le muestra los caminos de la vida y de la muerte.

El busca con santo amor salvar a la humanidad del pecado
  y de la indiferencia.

El juzga a los hombres y naciones con su recta voluntad
  declarada mediante los profetas y los apóstoles.

En Jesucristo, el hombre de Nazaret, nuestro Señor
      crucificado y resucitado,
  él ha morado entre nosotros
  y ha compartido nuestra condición común,
  venciendo al pecado y la muerte
  y reconciliando el mundo a sí.

El nos imparte su Santo Espíritu,
  creando y renovando la Iglesia de Jesucristo,
  uniendo en un pacto a los fieles de todas las edades,
      lenguas y razas.

El nos llama a su Iglesia
  a aceptar el precio y el gozo del discipulado,
  a ser sus siervos al servicio de los hombres,
  a proclamar el evangelio a todo el mundo
      y resistir el poder del mal,

a compartir el bautismo de Cristo y participar en su
Santa Cena,
a unirnos con él en su pasión y victoria.

El promete a todos los que en él confían
el perdón de los pecados y la plenitud de la gracia,
valor en la lucha por la justicia y la paz,
su presencia en la prueba y en el gozo,
y la vida eterna en su reino que no tiene fin.

A él sea la alabanza, la honra, la gloria y el poder. Amén.

Translated by Eduardo Guerra
Lycoming College, Pennsylvania

Ἡ Μαρτυρία τῆς Πίστεως

Πιστεύομεν εἰς θεόν, τὸ πνεύμα τὸ αἰώνιον,
τὸν πατέρα τοῦ κυρίου ἡμῶν Ἰησοῦ Χριστοῦ
καὶ πατέρα ἡμῶν, οὗ τοῖς ἔργοις διαμαρτυροῦμεν,

τὸν καλοῦντα τοὺς αἰῶνας εἰς τὸ εἶναι,
κτίζοντα τὸν ἄνθρωπον κατὰ τὸν ἴδιον εἰκόνα,
διδόντα πρὸ προσώπου αὐτοῦ τὰς ὁδοὺς τῆς τε ζωῆς καὶ τοῦ θανάτου,

τὸν δι᾽ ἀγάπης ἁγίας θέλοντα σώζειν πάντας ἀνθρώπους
ἀπὸ ματαιότητος καὶ ἁμαρτίας,

τὸν κρίνοντα ἀνθρώπους καὶ ἔθνη κατὰ τὸ θέλημα αὐτοῦ δίκαιον,
τὸ ἀπηγγελμένον διὰ προφητῶν καὶ ἀποστόλων,

ἐν Ἰησοῦ Χριστῷ τῷ ἀνθρώπῳ ἀπὸ Ναζαρέθ,
τῷ κυρίῳ ἡμῶν τῷ ἐσταυρωμένῳ καὶ ἐγηγερμένῳ,
τὸν ἐλθόντα εἰς ἡμᾶς
μετέχοντα τοῦ μέρους τοῦ κοινοῦ,
νικῶντα ἁμαρτίαν καὶ θάνατον
καὶ ἀποκαταλλάσσοντα τὸν κόσμον εἰς ἑαυτόν,

τὸν χαριζόμενον ἡμῖν τὸ πνεῦμα αὐτοῦ τὸ ἅγιον,
κτίζοντα καὶ ἀνακαινοῦντα τὴν ἐκκλησίαν Ἰησοῦ Χριστοῦ,
συνάγοντα ἐν διαθήκῃ λαὸν πιστὸν ἐκ πασῶν τῶν ἡλικιῶν
καὶ γλωσσῶν καὶ ἐκ παντὸς γένους ἀνθρώπων,

τὸν καλοῦντα ἡμᾶς εἰς τὴν ἐκκλησίαν αὐτοῦ
εἰς τὸ ἀναδέχεσθαι τὸ βάρος καὶ τὴν χαρὰν τοῦ μαθητὴν εἶναι,
εἰς τὸ εἶναι δούλους αὐτοῦ εἰς διακονίαν τῶν ἀνθρώπων,

131

εἰς τὸ καταγγέλλεσθαι τὸ εὐαγγέλιον παντὶ τῷ κόσμῳ
καὶ ἀνθίστασθαι ταῖς δυνάμεσι τοῦ πονηροῦ,
εἰς τὸ μετέχειν τοῦ βαπτίσματος τοῦ Χριστοῦ καὶ φαγεῖν
παρὰ τῆς τραπέζης αὐτοῦ,
εἰς τὸ κοινωνεῖν αὐτῷ ἐν τοῖς παθήμασι αὐτοῦ καὶ ἐν τῇ νίκῃ,

τὸν ἐπαγγέλλοντα πᾶσι τοῖς πιστεύουσιν ἐπ᾽ αὐτῷ
ἄφεσιν ἁμαρτιῶν καὶ περισσείαν χάριτος,
παρρησίαν ἐπὶ τῷ ἀγῶνι περὶ δικαιοσύνης καὶ εἰρήνης,
παρουσίαν αὐτοῦ ἐν πειρασμῷ καὶ ἀγαλλιάσει
καὶ ζωὴν αἰώνιον ἐν τῇ βασιλείᾳ αὐτοῦ τῇ ἀφθάρτῳ.

Αὐτῷ ἡ εὐλογία καὶ ἡ τιμὴ καὶ ἡ δόξα καὶ τὸ κράτος. Ἀμήν.

Translated by Robert V. Moss, Jr.
Lancaster Theological Seminary, Pennsylvania